Now you tell me!

12
ARMY
WIVES
GIVE THE
BEST ADVICE
THEY NEVER
GOT

Other Books in the Series:

Now You Tell Me! 12 Actors Give the Best Advice They Never Got

Now You Tell Me! 12 College Students Give the Best Advice They Never Got

Now you tell me!

12 ARMY WIVES GIVE THE BEST ADVICE THEY NEVER GOT

SHERIDAN SCOTT
DONNA LYONS • B.K. SHERER

Arundel Publishing
36 Crystal Farm Rd.
Warwick, NY 10990
www.arundelpublishing.com
www.nowyoutellmebooks.com

ISBN 978-1-933608-31-0
First Edition December 2012
Printed in the United States of America

TABLE OF CONTENTS

Now you tell me!

12 ARMY WIVES GIVE THE BEST ADVICE THEY NEVER GOT

PROLOGUE

BETH CHIARELLI

"Don't over-identify with what your husband is doing. Let him do his thing and you do yours."

The Army was Beth Chiarelli's life for over forty years as her husband Peter progressed from second lieutenant to four-star general. Beth and Peter met in 1968 during their freshman year at Seattle University in Washington State. Beth was not from a military family and didn't know Pete was in ROTC when they started dating. She majored in community services and went on to use those skills on behalf of the Army community as her husband held each level of command from platoon to corps. Peter recently retired, having concluded his career serving four years as the second-highest-ranking general in the Army. Beth and Peter have three children, Peter, Erin and Patrick.

1

IN THE BEGINNING

I was totally clueless about the Army when I met Pete. He seemed like a normal person; I didn't even see him in uniform for quite a while. Of course, this was back in the 1960s when feelings ran high about Vietnam; Army Reserve units used to get bomb threats and the ROTC students didn't dare wear their uniforms on campus. It was very different from today.

Pete and I never had a conversation in which he said, "I'm going to be in the Army as a career. This is what I want to do." If I had understood more about the Army, the fact that he was so committed to ROTC would have been a clue. At the time, I didn't have any idea.

We got engaged at the beginning of our senior year and married after graduation. Pete was commissioned, and we headed to Fort Knox for his officer basic training. At the time, a student commissioned by the ROTC could probably satisfy his obligation to the Army in three years because Vietnam was dying down and they were letting people go. But we liked it and decided to stay.

MAKING A LIVING

IF YOU WANT SOMETHING, ASK FOR IT

Our first assignment after the Basic Course was Fort Lewis, which probably contributed to our decision to stay in. It was close to home, and we were there for five years. How we got there is a lesson in how the Army can work for you, if you ask the right questions. A major came to the Basic Course and talked to the students about their assignments. He said, "If you have any questions about your assignment, give me a call." His name was Major Shaw, and I'd love to meet him again sometime. Pete got orders for Fort Bliss, and we were both so naïve about assignments we said, "It would be so much better if we could go to Fort Lewis because it's so close to home."

I said, "That major said to call him if you had any questions."

> **If you want something, ask for it. The worst that can happen is they say "No."**

Sure enough, Pete called him on Wednesday and said, "We'd like to go to Fort Lewis." That Friday Major Shaw called back and said a position just opened at Fort Lewis—so we got new orders!

Later in Pete's career we would learn that it isn't always that easy to change assignments. But we did learn an important lesson at that point: if you want something, ask for it. The worst that can happen is they say "No."

EARLY LESSONS IN ARMY POLITICS

We arrived at Fort Lewis and Pete was assigned to 3rd of the 5th Cavalry Battalion. He was a brand new second lieutenant working with aviators who were older and had served in Vietnam. We were newly married, and they accepted us as the little brother and sister of the group.

After Pete was promoted to first lieutenant, a captain was relieved of his company command (that's what the Army calls getting fired) because one of his tanks kind of leveled an apple orchard in Yakima, Washington. Pete was selected to take over, even though he was not yet a captain. This was my first experience with professional jealousy. His selection jumped him over some other officers who were hoping to be company commanders. This would have been a career-building thing for these guys just back from Vietnam. Now they were passed over for this young guy, and there were some hurt feelings that spilled into our social life.

At the time, I didn't have a clue what any of that was about. All I knew was suddenly I was invited to go to everything. I was on the list to go to the Colonel's house and to this event and that one. But a couple of the spouses from the battalion were treating me differently, as if we were no longer friends, and I couldn't figure out why. When I said something to Pete, he explained that some of these guys had been to Vietnam two or three times and didn't get to command troops. That helped me understand why they might be upset, and while I couldn't change the career situation, I could do my best not to cause any further ill feelings. So I treated them like nothing had changed in our relationship, and was careful not to mention attending gatherings at the Colonel's house.

HANDLING DEPLOYMENT AS A SENIOR SPOUSE

My husband deployed twice to Iraq. The first time was in 2004, when he was the Division Commander for 1st Cavalry Division. The second time was in 2006, when he served as the Commander for Multi-National Corps-Iraq.

The first deployment was particularly hard. This was after the first big wave of combat operations in Iraq. All of the talk was that they were going over to replace the sewer system, restore electricity and provide potable water—to rebuild Baghdad.

They had barely gotten there, hadn't even officially taken over, when we lost eight soldiers. It was chaos. Nobody is ever ready for that. Nobody.

Before you know it, back home, we had to plan memorials for seventeen people. We started having these huge memorials every month. It became surreal. Now, sadly, it's very ordinary, but then it wasn't. It seemed bizarre that we would have to have them.

I felt horrible for the chaplains back here at Fort Hood because every month for these mass memorial ceremonies they had to try to come up with something cogent to say that was new, or at least had a different twist, for wave after wave of newly bereaved families. It was very sad.

Some of the brigade commanders' wives also had a very difficult time. They could go to each memorial ceremony, but they could not handle going back and talking to family members afterward. I supported their decisions. I always said, if that is not your thing, if it's not something with which you're comfortable, do not go back to visit the families. Don't force it if you can't handle it. It doesn't help anyone.

I felt the same way when they started creating Care Teams to visit the families of deceased soldiers. This is not for everybody. It is *absolutely* not for everybody. This is stuff that will affect you for the rest of your life, so don't think this is something that you have to do if you can't handle it, emotionally or spiritually or mentally.

That first deployment was not an easy time for me, personally. My mother died in December, Pete left in March, and then we started losing soldiers. I was not in a good place at all. Anybody who knew me would see me out and about doing things and think I was holding up just fine. But I would come home and break down there. It was like I made an appointment to cry when I was alone, to just get it out of my system.

Fortunately, I had wonderful support from the people around me. Our youngest, Patrick, was a senior in high school and at home with me. I also had terrific support from Pam Metz, the Corps Commander's wife, and Linda Odierno, wife of the 4th Infantry Division Commander. We were all neighbors and have remained dear friends to this day.

Christmas that year was really tough. I don't remember a thing about that day except that I knew I just had to get through it. After my mother's recent death, so many soldier losses, and with my husband still deployed to an increasingly dangerous combat zone, I didn't feel like celebrating the holiday. I had to wake up and just make it through. I was grateful I didn't have little kids. I had wonderful, supportive older kids who understood why—with my mother gone and Pete on such a dangerous tour, with so many soldiers lost, so many families in grief—it was such a difficult day.

Earlier in the month I did have a huge division Christmas party at the house. Some people were surprised, but I knew I had to do something to acknowledge the season and keep spirits up. It turned out to be a good thing; everyone had fun. The next year, Dee Thurman (whose husband had taken over 4th Infantry Division) said, "I'm doing exactly what you did. I'm having a party. Even if my husband is gone, I'm having a party!" I had some really wonderful people around me.

VISITING FAMILIES OF THE FALLEN

I always went back to the reception for the family members after memorial ceremonies. My biggest fear was being viewed as insincere because I didn't know who they were or their relation to the soldier. The Rear Detachment representative was behind me trying to give a heads up about who I was talking to, but often a family was not where you expected them to be, and names would get confused. So, I learned to say, "Tell me about your soldier," because this encouraged them to tell me about their loved one. They could be the mother, the cousin, the wife, anything. And best of all, it gave them permission to talk. I still use that today. Because I still want to hear. I really do.

The other officers' wives and I learned a lot about dealing with people who have experienced great loss. By the time we were about seven months into the deployment, we would say, "I wish we didn't know so much about memorials."

SUPPORTING OTHER SPOUSES

April 4th is a day emblazoned on everybody's mind. That was the day 1st Cavalry Division lost those first eight soldiers in Iraq. Since I was the

Division Commander's wife, when my husband's headquarters sent the word back to Fort Hood that we had lost those soldiers, I felt strongly about supporting the brigade commanders' wives, but not doing their jobs for them. When there are deaths in a brigade, the brigade commander's spouse has a lot of responsibility helping take care of hurting families and representing her husband (who is deployed) at the memorial ceremony. When Pete had been a brigade commander I had done all those things, so I was tempted to do that now. I was not the brigade senior spouse any longer, but I was in a position to provide support for them. It took me awhile to learn how to provide support as the Division Commander's wife, though, because back when Pete was a brigade commander at Fort Lewis, we didn't have a division over us, so there was no division commander's spouse for me to observe. I had to figure it out on my own, but I did.

Eventually I understood that there is not just one way to do things. Each brigade spouse has a different personality, and I needed to encourage each one to do what needed to be done in her or his own way. To a person, the spouses were fabulous. They were each very, very different from one another, but they each stepped up when needed.

FAMILY READINESS GROUPS

The one point where I stepped in and took control was on the subject of Family Readiness Support Assistants (FRSAs). The Army had just created a new program for hiring people to help the Family Readiness Group (FRG) leaders with all of the administrative issues it takes to run an FRG so the leaders would be free to run the groups. But you can't imagine how many battalion commanders' wives just fought that tooth and nail. I finally said at one meeting, "They are hiring people to find meeting space and provide child care—everything you hate doing! What could be better than that?" But these particular women really wanted to be "queen bee" in their unit, to micromanage *everything*. That didn't fly with me at all.

I flat out said, "This is just the way it is now. We are not paying these people so you can try to trump everything they do. You need to help these people."

And, pretty much, I made sure that was that.

BRING POSITIVE ENERGY TO AN FRG MEETING

Whenever I lead a spouses group, I always assume those who attend the meetings are there because they want to be, not because someone has twisted their arms. I make it clear to the group that since there are no longer comments about officers' wives on their husbands' evaluation reports, you do not have to be here. I assume that if you are at an FRG meeting, you *want* to be here.

The reverse is also true. If you don't want to help with the unit, don't come—otherwise you'll share that negative energy with everybody else. If you are here because you want to be here, then hopefully you will leave with some information that will make your life easier. I don't know everything, but I am in a position to find things out more easily. Maybe I can help you skip a few steps. So let me help you.

RESILIENT, FLEXIBLE, UNFLAPPABLE

Throughout Pete's career, I was often put in leadership roles. I'm a resilient person, like my mother, and I'm able to handle a lot of stuff. I could always get along with Pete's bosses, and their wives would often sit me next to the complicated people because I could figure out how to talk with them. "She's such a pill," they would say, "would you sit by her?"

Thankfully, my personality was well suited for what we did. At first I wondered, "Am I flexible or just spineless? Am I just willing to go wherever I'm sent?"

I've come to think this is an important attribute for the spouse of a senior leader. Never over-identify with what your husband is doing. Let him do his thing, and you do yours. There are perks of being the wife of a senior leader, of course, but there's responsibility as well. For example, I had access to more information because of the meetings I attended and always felt a responsibility to share it.

I have been around women who knew their husband's exact date of rank, who could tell you exactly who should be in the picture, and who always knew exactly where they fit in the protocol of the situation. Frankly, it used to make me laugh. We came into the military just at the very tail end of the old Army. There were still some stories about commanders' wives who wanted you to wear gloves and hats and all that stuff. It was kind of fun to watch as the old met up with the new, but some people didn't take to it very well.

TRADITIONS WORTH KEEPING

Still, you hate to see *all* the traditions die away. Some of them are worth keeping. I think a wonderful tradition that doesn't happen often today is making an old fashioned call on people. You learn a lot if you just visit, one on one, instead of always meeting in big groups. I always tried, when Pete was in command mode, to have lunch individually with each of the other commanders' wives. This can be a great way to get to know their personalities. It is important to pay attention to the individual so you can support them without telling them what to do. Certainly, if anyone had told me what to do, I would not have reacted well!

At times it was pretty evident what needed to be done, but things worked much better if I encouraged them to figure out how to do it and own the process and the result.

MAKING A LIFE

CATTLE CALL IN THE OBSTETRICS WING

Our first child, Peter, was born in 1974 while we were stationed at Fort Lewis. When you are having your first baby, you think you are the only person having a baby, but looking back, there was a huge baby boom in the Army after troops returned from Vietnam. There were twenty-eight babies born the same night I had Peter! Doctor's appointments were like cattle calls. I remember this nurse poking her head around the corner, "Anybody who has gained more than five pounds since their last meeting, you must see a doctor rather than just have your vitals taken."

> If you are nice and treat people right, they will take care of you.

Then she looks around the corner again and says, "Well, it's crowded today, anybody gaining more than seven pounds since their last appointment?"

It seemed crazy, and my mother and sister were horrified when I would tell them these stories. But in the end I was luckier than most. I developed a real connection with one of the doctors. I liked him and he related to me. He greased it so my last three months I only saw him. I wasn't trying to buck the system, but I was learning that you don't have to accept being just a face in the crowd. If you are nice and treat people right, they will take care of you. Then sure enough, my doctor happened to be on duty the night that I went into labor and delivered my first son. Now that was wonderful.

The birth of my second child was the reverse of the first. For the first one I had just the perfect doctor in the most hideous hospital ever. The second was born in a civilian hospital, which was a much more glamorous facility, but the doctor was just horrible. In spite of that, I was happy to be there because Pete had just graduated from his Advanced Course and we were staying with my parents. I got to bring the baby home to where I had grown up.

I don't waste time trying to compare the Army and civilian medical systems. There are good points and bad points to every situation, so I figure you accept wherever you are and make the best of it.

KIDS AND THE ARMY LIFE

We always told the kids that they were the experts when it comes to growing up in the Army. We never had to go through the things they did, so Pete and I always tried to encourage them to share their feelings. I would say they did extremely well. Our oldest remembers that his years of elementary school were fairly normal, because his father was in graduate school and teaching at West Point. If asked at that time what his father did, he would have said "professor."

Then, when he was in sixth grade, we moved to Germany and it was "game on." His father was gone most of the time, new baby in the house, living in a foreign country . . . welcome to "real" Army life!

But all three children look back on it and love that they grew up in such a diverse population. They felt much more prepared for college. They felt more worldly than some of the people they went to school with. When we lived in a German village, Peter had to take this dumb bus for an hour and a half to get to school. It was a real pain, and I didn't like that he had to do it, but he did fine. We always had a lot of people in the house, hosting unit parties, staff functions, community leaders, and the three of them learned to be really good at social situations. We took advantage of the local landscapes and did ski vacations and a lot of other great family stuff wherever we were stationed.

If any of my kids had really suffered because of our Army life, I don't think we could have stayed in. I would have called it quits. Pete always said it was my call—he was like that. I can remember friends of mine whose kids really did suffer. If someone had a child who was very shy and did not easily make friends, that child was extremely unhappy every time they moved. I couldn't have done that. I couldn't have looked at my kids and said, "Well, this is what your dad does, so this is how it has to be. You just gotta suck it up." But I didn't have to. Our children handled everything very well.

> We don't want the world to feel sorry for military kids, but we want the world to understand that they've got a few extra rocks in their backpack. It's important to recognize that they are serving too.

I always watched for any hints that I was too involved in community stuff and not working for the benefit of my own family. I remember when Erin was in second grade and Peter in fifth grade, there were two pumpkin pies on the counter.

Erin said, "I love pumpkin pie!"

Peter responded, "They're probably for somebody else."

I thought, "Take a note." That changed how I did things from then on.

It's not the easiest thing to be a military child. At the Military Child Education Coalition, we say, "We don't want the world to feel sorry for military kids, but we want the world to understand that they've got a few extra rocks in their backpack. It's important to recognize that they are serving too."

My kids have served their country as we moved around, just by being the great kids they are.

DEPLOYMENT REUNIONS AND CHILDREN

I feel very strongly that when your husband returns from a deployment it is not right to pull the kids out of school for two weeks just to spend time with him. How would you ever convince your children that their lives are important if they have worked hard preparing for a school play or recital, then you yank them out, saying, "Just because Dad's home, we're going to take a two-week vacation."

I tried to dissuade people from doing that. I found that giving kids half days to be away from school seemed to work as a good substitute. Now all the research agrees with me, suggesting that when a parent returns from a deployment keeping kids in their normal routine is absolutely key to their adjustment. It just didn't make sense to me that we should send the message that the only person who matters is your dad. I think if you are going to teach kids to value what they are doing, you can't just yank them out of school.

READUSTING TO EACH OTHER

Pete is a pretty resilient person, so he didn't have a lot of issues readjusting to life back home after the deployment. The biggest adjustment for me came after spending a whole year planning my own days and controlling my schedule, now I had to adjust to "Oh, wait ten more minutes; I gotta make one more call."

Before you get too frustrated, remind yourself, "This is a good thing. My schedule is not as important as the fact that he's back. I'm glad he's back!" But it does take some patience, it really does. I have to say we were pretty successful readjusting, but it didn't hurt that we had been together a long, long time before he deployed.

REST AND RELAXATION

When they worked out the R&R leave schedules for the division headquarters in Iraq, it turned out that October would be the best time for Pete to take leave. Unfortunately, Patrick was a freshman in college, and would have just started a few weeks before. It would have been a terrible time for him to take a break, yet if he didn't and his father was home, he would be so distracted. So I told Pete, "You and I will meet in Ireland."

That way there wasn't even a chance that Patrick would be tempted to leave school. It turned out Pete and I had a really nice trip, and it was the right decision for Patrick as well.

FRIENDS AND MENTORS

I have had some wonderful mentors through the years. Usually, the mentors were women who were about ten years older than me. These were women I could talk to when I was having problems with a difficult spouse and who kept me sane when everything seemed to be falling apart.

As we traveled the world, I also developed some long lasting friendships. When we were stationed in Germany, Pete's parents came over so they could meet the new grandchild (our third child). While they were visiting, Pete's dad died. It was a nightmare. During this time my husband had responsibilities with the Canadian Army Trophy Competition, so he was gone a lot. It was horrible.

But somehow the worst situations breed the deepest friendships, and my friends didn't let me down. They were just incredible. These are the times when you just bond with people like crazy. They helped me get through that tough time, so I have remained particularly close to that group of people. Sometimes you will have experiences with your friends that bond you so closely you believe you'll never have friends like that again. But then you move on, and somehow you find new ones.

YOU WILL NOT BELIEVE WHAT YOU DID

When Pete took the "Vice" job (Vice Chief of Staff of the Army), my kids asked me how many times we had moved. I counted up, and this was our twenty-ninth house. Over the years I changed my approach to unpacking.

Usually, you're tempted to do the kitchen first, and everything else later. After about ten years, I started doing my bedroom first, because every day you wake up and it's nice. You don't feel so defeated when you wake up. I can't say I did that every time, but the times I did I really liked it.

We unpack fast, and Pete became the perfect helper. I would tell him, "I just need manpower, I don't want any suggestions." I knew I had his attention for a week or ten days, and then I wouldn't have it once he went back to work. He was good about giving me what he could. Twice I had to do a move by myself—to Texas, and also moving out of Belgium. That was busy!

When we moved to Gelnhausen, Germany, it was total chaos. We'd been given a house, but at the last minute, they made a decision to let the Command Sergeant Major move onto post. They literally gave him our house as we were on the plane flying over. When we arrived, there was nothing they could do but put us in temporary quarters, where we stayed from August to the end of October.

I had to leave my kids playing with people we had just met so I could go house hunting. These people were fine, but I wasn't. It was so stressful. Then one day I came back to discover that my son had fallen out of a swing and broken both of his arms. There he was in Frankfurt with the battalion commander's wife, and these huge plaster casts, and Pete had to take off for a training exercise in Grafenwoehr, Germany. I didn't have my European driver's license yet—and then I found out I was having a baby. Could it get any crazier?

I always tell the younger wives, when you look back, you will not believe you did what you did. You just will not believe it. But the thing is, you are in a culture, the Army culture, where other people are doing the same stuff all the time. When you try to tell your civilian friends, they are just horrified. They think it's crazy, and maybe it is.

Germany was a very stressful time, but we got through it. Now that my son is the same age we were at the time (which blows his mind) and has two little kids of his own, he says, "I cannot believe what you did when we got to Germany, and Dad just disappeared."

> **If you have an expectation that somehow your husband's job, or the house or the quarters that you get will make you somehow different, it's not that way.**

UNREALISTIC EXPECTATIONS

I think some women have the expectation that their husbands' jobs and promotions will supply something they're lacking in themselves. As I described it during a talk to a group of young women, "Every time I move away I find myself again." You are who *you* are. Your personality is going to stay the same. So if you have an expectation that somehow your husband's job, or the house or the quarters that you get will make you somehow different, it's not that way. At the end of the day, it's still you making decisions.

LIFE OF A GENERAL OFFICER

When we first came into the Army, Pete and I didn't have much. We rented a television for $6 a month. It makes me laugh to think about those days. You'd think that by the time you make general you are beyond living like that. Not so. Let me tell you how funny it was. We were in Belgium, living in a hotel while waiting for Pete to be promoted to general. We finally moved into this crummy, crummy house, on SHAPE (Supreme Headquarters Allied Powers Europe, a multinational headquarters located in Mons, Belgium). Pete was doing the job that would be his as general, but he still hadn't pinned on the rank yet.

They gave us a date for his promotion, and we made plans, including buying a plane ticket for Pete's mother. Then the powers that be decided another officer needed to be promoted before Pete, and changed the date. So we ate the ticket.

Pete pinned on a couple of months later. So he was finally a general, and we lived in the crummiest house with this stinky plumbing problem and broken, temporary furniture. It did not feel too special, let me tell you. The Kosovo war was about to happen, and he did shift work. He used to leave at six o'clock at night and come home at six o'clock in the morning. When he walked through the door, I would say "Hey, General, welcome to your palace!" It was insane. It was really hilarious. Just because you are a general, or a general's spouse, doesn't mean you should expect special treatment.

There is also an interesting dynamic to relationships with others at the senior level. Here is the bottom line: no matter what the situation is, you have to make the effort to get along with all the other generals and their wives. You don't have to be best friends, but it upsets the applecart too much if you can't get along. If you don't, that tension becomes palpable, people can feel it. It can really do a number on a unit. If there is tension like that, take the high road. Don't make it worse.

Another thing I've learned is, when you are doing errands or business out in the community, make it a point to get along with everybody. You never know where you might run into the bank teller, or grocer or physician again. If you go to the bank and tear somebody's head off because he didn't do what you thought he was supposed to do, you will probably end up sitting next to him at dinner some time, and it's uncomfortable. When you are in a leadership position, you are supposed to be a "community leader." It's far better to get along than to try to mend fences.

Whatever the situation, give it your best shot.

PARTING ADVICE

Whatever the situation, give it your own best shot. You can find something wrong with any situation. There will always be some issue to face. Sometimes you have to decide what your own happiness is going to be. It doesn't matter if you are military or civilian; there will be some hard times. Probably the worst thing for me was having to tell our son who was going to be a high school senior that he had to move. But we had made the decision as a family that we weren't going to split up. Some families, for the sake of their kids' potential college careers, left them behind when they moved. For some that worked out great, others not. But still, you have to follow your gut for your own family. Make your decisions, and live with them.

I think, in the end, the best symbolism for Army life is the change of command ceremony. You walk on the field the day your husband takes command, and you hope you can do your best in this new stage and keep it together until the day it's over and time to move on.

Pete and I really enjoyed our Army lives. But those days are over, and we've walked onto the next "field." We are very happy doing what we are doing. We don't look back.

12
ARMY
WIVES

FRANCES SASSER

"Being flexible is key."

Frances Sasser grew up in a strict, single parent home in Fayetteville, North Carolina. She married Charles Sasser Jr., her high school sweetheart, who needed permission from his parents to join the military at age seventeen.

Charles is now Division Command Sergeant Major at Fort Riley, Kansas. Not only has he deployed four times so far, Frances has now watched her son deploy two times as well.

Frances graduated with a bachelor's degree in business management in June 2011. A strong woman, she learned the ropes the good old fashioned way with hard work, love of military and family.

IN THE BEGINNING

I was born in Fayetteville, North Carolina. Fayetteville is a military town; home of the 82nd Airborne Division at Fort Bragg. My sister and I were raised by my mother, on her own. She had came to the United States around 1960 from Germany; at the time, she did not know any English.

Charles and I met during our junior year in high school. He was a young man who knew what he wanted: to join the Army and to marry me. He proposed, and we were married shortly after our senior year. By then he had already signed the paperwork to enlist.

His ASVAB (Armed Services Vocational Aptitude Battery) test scores were high enough that he could have had any job. (The ASVAB measures abilities in math, science, reading comprehension, and mechanical skills, and helps predict the academic and occupational success of military recruits.)

Somehow, Charles knew that he wanted to be in the Infantry. All these years later, after seeing him flourish in his career, I know that he made the right decision. He was born to be in the Infantry.

At the time, I didn't know what being an Army wife meant or what was involved. But I did know that this guy I loved had all the drive to carry us, and how could I not support that? Since those humble beginnings I've seen many things in the military change and change again. I think the biggest lesson I've learned is that being flexible is key (and a little humor doesn't hurt).

MAKING A LIVING

NEW WIFE ON THE BLOCK

My first experience as an Army spouse was in November 1984. Charles had just finished basic training and Advanced Infantry Training (AIT) at Fort Benning, Georgia, and our duty station was Fort Stewart, Georgia. I'd been on post at Fort Bragg, back in North Carolina, many times. This, however, was my first time shopping at the commissary and Post Exchange (PX) as a wife and mother.

We had a sponsor who welcomed us and showed us around. Usually assigned by the commander, sponsors are people who are usually of an equal rank and have already been in the unit for a while, so they're able to help new families get settled quickly. I quickly learned where all the important facilities were, such as the gas station, the hospital, the commissary and the PX. (The commissary sells grocery items and the exchanges carry consumer goods.) I learned the hard way that you need to present a military member ID card or military family member ID card when entering the store or paying for goods.

Being flexible is key (and a little humor doesn't hurt).

I remember feeling like everyone else was moving at the speed of light handling their business, and I was the only person who didn't really quite know how to do things. People weren't very friendly or willing to help the newbie figure things out. Maybe that's just how it seemed; I was only eighteen and pregnant, and facing new challenges every day. I felt overwhelmed and very much out of the loop.

Over time I learned the ropes, and it became easier. However, I kept that memory; through the years, it helped me become willing to stop and help young wives who looked completely at sea.

EDUCATE YOURSELF!

New families entering the military have so many resources available to them. More so than when I was a young military spouse. Take advantage of those resources and educate yourself about military customs and

Perhaps the most important thing to do—as soon as possible after arrival—is to make friends with a spouse in the unit, or even a neighbor, who has an outlook and interests similar to yours.

traditions. The military language is a beast to tackle, but if you arm yourself with the basics it helps you better understand what's going on, and also helps you get through Army life. The Army Community Service (ACS) program is a great way for young military spouses to learn Army language and lots more. There are different levels of training that help with rank recognition, acronyms and even military protocol. You can learn it all online now; isn't technology grand? The truth is, it's an ongoing life course. My husband has been in the Army for twenty-seven years now, and I'm still learning things.

When your husband talks to you about his job, show interest! It's important for him and important for you. I can guarantee you that along the way you will be asked about your husband's unit, known as a Military Occupation Specialty (MOS). I've run into wives who have no clue! It's his profession, and a good part of your life, so at least be informed and understand what's going on.

It's also a good idea to take a tour of post. All posts have a newcomer's orientation these days, and the tour helps you know where the important facilities are.

Perhaps the most important thing to do—as soon as possible after arrival—is to make friends with a spouse in the unit, or even a neighbor, who has an outlook and interests similar to yours.

Realize that gossip can and will be abundant. Steer clear! Nothing good ever comes from it.

The best advice that I can give to families new to the military is that being flexible is key. Things change constantly and the more you fight it, the harder it will be to have a positive attitude. The military does *not* have a conspiracy to ruin your life or to make it difficult. The Army tries really hard to make military life more enjoyable, steadily improving the quality of life for everyone.

THE SECRET TO HANDLING A MOVE

The secret to handling a move is organization, organization, and a little more organization.

While Charles handled all the logistics when we had a permanent change of station (PCS), I would immediately organize rooms, declutter, downsize and clean before we began packing.

I would also set up things on the other end, such as the cable and phone. I am a huge advocate for attention to detail. I make lists and prioritize things that need to be done, and this has always helped me in the past. Along the way, you get better and faster, and it almost becomes second nature.

Things change constantly and the more you fight it, the harder it will be to have a positive attitude. The military does *not* have a conspiracy to ruin your life.

Another piece of advice: Always be at least three steps ahead. You never know what may come in your path, but at least you'll be armed if your plan somehow goes awry. For example, be sure to pack enough clothes while your life is being shipped around the world—just in case everything doesn't show up on the other end. Think about what it's like to go on a trip and have to buy clothes if your luggage is lost. If you are unprepared, this could be a burden financially and otherwise.

Always take people up on an offer to help.

Another tip—always take people up on an offer to help. You can't be everything to everyone, and there is power in numbers. Whether helping pack at your old place, or welcoming you to your new place, when people offer help, say, "Yes, please!"

I have always had neighbors (whether on post or off) welcome me to the area. With that usually comes an offer to help with something: kids, pets, or even unpacking.

SETTLE IN

Settling quickly into your new place helps your life tremendously. There's nothing more frustrating than trying to manage day-to-day activities while still living out of boxes. I always organize (there's that word again) each room before the packers come so that when things are packed they are in the room they belong, which is much easier when unpacking.

On the other end, always unpack the kitchen first, along with the master bedroom. Then take care of the kids' rooms. The living room will come soon enough. Remember, everyone has to eat and sleep—go for the necessities first! I can happily say I have this down to a science now.

EACH DEPLOYMENT IS DIFFERENT

Charles has been deployed four times since 9/11, and he will deploy again. People may think that it gets easier, but each deployment is different.

Different for him, as he has had different jobs during each deployment, and his responsibility increases as he gets promoted. He is in charge of a larger number of troops, which is a heavy burden when there are casualties.

Different for me, in that I've been in different places in my life as a person.

During Charles' first deployment, our daughter had just left home. It seemed extra hard trying to make things "normal" for our fifteen-year-old son who missed his sister and needed his dad.

During Charles' second deployment, our son had left for basic training, and I was alone in the house. Even though I had many friends around me, I was a new empty-nester; my "baby" was gone as well as my husband. I also had to move alone from Hawaii to Colorado. I had never done that before, but I knew that I could. I've always been resilient!

The next time, I was a full-time college student in a new place.

This last one was the ultimate: My son and husband were both being deployed at the same time.

Another deployment looms as I write this. It will surely be different. I'm not sure how yet, but it will.

I could not have done any of this without my Army sisters. They are truly the backbone of our lives. We are each other's lifeline.

Keep your Army sisters close, and keep phone numbers, necessary paperwork (insurance information, wills, power of attorney) where you can easily find it!

REUNITING WITH YOUR LOVED ONE

Reunions can be just as stressful as the beginning of a deployment. This is a time when families reunite. It's also a time when your loved one integrates back into your normal routine. This time will have its share of challenges as a new normal is created. The spouses that have spent the last year handling everything are now expected to step back and let the men take charge again. This is hard to do when we're the ones who have been running things while our soldiers have been deployed.

Reunions can be just as stressful as the beginning of a deployment.

But our men need to feel needed. Each of them still wants to be the man of the house, and believe it or not, they've missed taking out the trash. That normalcy is important for their transition as well as ours.

I don't like planning big reunions with extended family members. This may sound terrible, but they don't live with us on a daily basis, and a call to let them know your soldier is home safely will do for now. A few months after he comes home, we do meet up with extended family for a short visit.

WHEN A CHILD DEPLOYS

We have a daughter, Amanda, age twenty-seven, and a son, Sean, who is twenty-four.

A sergeant with two deployments under his belt, Sean is an Army interrogator currently stationed at Schofield Barracks, Hawaii.

Having my son deploy was different from having my husband deploy. My husband, a Command Sergeant Major, had a security team with him. Although his safety was not guaranteed, I had less to worry about. My son, on the other hand, was only an SPC (Specialist) and more likely to be closer to the trenches—since SPCs are the security. I went through a period when they were both deployed at the same time; in two different wars—Iraq and Afghanistan.

I got a notification call from the Department of Defense (DOD), something no one ever wants. Sean was involved in an incident on August 7, 2010, and he received a Purple Heart. His forward operating base (FOB Kalsu) was attacked, and his girlfriend, Specialist Faith Hinkley, was killed and his friend Sergeant Carson was badly wounded and also received a Purple Heart. The three of them worked closely together on a daily basis. I had met this sweet girl, Faith, just weeks before when she came home for her mid-tour leave. I know that Sean would gladly return that Purple Heart to have Faith back. It is an ongoing struggle emotionally for him and for our family. I cannot quite imagine what struggles the Hinkley family endures daily. I keep them all in my thoughts and prayers constantly.

When I heard the news, my heart sank. I felt badly for her family and wondered what they were doing at that very moment. We met Faith's family at her funeral, and we have since been back to visit. They also invited us to their family gathering to remember and celebrate her life on the one-year anniversary of her death. We felt very honored. The Hinkley family is a great example of love and strength.

It's incredibly important that we be there for each other during these times; things can and will happen. Keep a support base of family and friends very close in good and bad times.

HAVE PERSONAL GOALS DURING DEPLOYMENTS

Through all these deployments, I've learned that you can choose to be miserable or be happy. I choose to be happy, and I work at having goals to get me through.

During Charles' deployment when we were at Fort Carson, Colorado, a good friend and my "battle buddy" helped us keep our bodies strong by setting goals. Our group had two large goals. The first was to hike up Pike's Peak, which, at 14,110 feet, was quite an accomplishment. At the time, I was a full-time student, bogged down with a heavy study load. Because of this, I never completed that goal and regret it to this day. I was at least able to do several shorter hikes, and the social time along with the workout turned out to be a very important part of the process.

> Through all these deployments, I've learned that you can choose to be miserable or be happy.

Our second goal was to run a half-marathon. I did complete that goal and have the medal to prove it. Our group trained together, and those are some wonderful memories of a time when my life was difficult. Army wives stick together, and those friendships are still strong and still growing.

MAKING A LIFE

LIVING: ON OR OFF POST?

Typically we have lived off post, but whenever we did I really missed the camaraderie. Still, we made the choice to live off post because early in our military career, housing was very small, and we felt so cramped. (We always seemed to have a lot of furniture.)

I also wanted our kids to mingle with civilian kids as well as military kids. I think we made the right decision. They still keep in touch with some of those civilian friends to this day.

Go with the flow! Things change all the time, and if you are unable to adapt, things can be challenging. Also, having a positive attitude is desirable. I am drawn to those people who are positive and upbeat. Realizing that things change and being able to cope accordingly helps.

SCHOOLS

When it comes to moves, it is critically important to keep your kids included in the process!

Our family always grabbed the kids' school transitions by the horns. As soon as we knew that we were moving, we would communicate that to our kids and include them in making family plans to travel around that area to learn much as we could. We always collected as much information as possible about the schools they would attend.

When it comes to moves, it is critically important to keep your kids included in the process!

Although it has not been always been easy for them, kids are resilient. I feel that our kids, now that they're grown, can adapt in most situations better because of their moving experiences.

ME TIME

Becoming an Army wife so young meant no college education right after high school. In fact, I didn't get my degree until June 2011! I graduated from Colorado Technical University in Colorado Springs, earning a bachelor's degree in business management, with honors. My plan is to continue toward my MBA when time allows. Kids, PCSs, and life got in the way, but I realized that after our youngest left the house, there was no good reason for me not to continue and fulfill that goal. So I did.

The added bonus was that my grown children told me how proud they were of me.

Finally, I did something for me.

DON'T HAVE EXPECTATIONS

Some civilians think because military families get moving companies to relocate us, paid medical care and money for housing, that things are handed to us and we have it easy. Anyone who's actually been in a military family knows this has to be the hardest life. But you know what? I wouldn't trade it for the world. I've actually come to like moving every few years, experiencing different cultures and being able to see the world.

I think the biggest mistake I made was putting everyone else's needs before mine.

The truth is, I would support my husband no matter what he decided to do for a career; we just happen to be in the military.

The biggest downside of the military life, in my view, has been the time Charles and I have spent apart from each other. It definitely wears on a relationship. Communication is key!

I think the biggest mistake I made was putting everyone else's needs before mine. It is hard for a young wife to be able to balance all that is expected of her while raising a family. I wish that I had continued with my education back in my early twenties, but I let excuses get in the way. Years later, I put myself first and finished my bachelor's degree.

I would tell young wives that they shouldn't feel guilty about saying no sometimes. You cannot be everything to everyone. It's okay to let some things fall by the wayside.

WHAT I KNOW NOW

Even with all that I know now, I would still marry a soldier—my soldier. I am around a great group of people, and we all share a bond that cannot be broken. I always tell young military wives that they should never be intimidated by senior spouses. There is always a lesson to learn from them and their experiences. Understand the commonality you all share is that you love and support a soldier. If you begin with that, you're off to a great start.

MELODY CHARLES

"Dual military couples understand the pressures on each other."

Melody Charles grew up in Waterloo, Iowa. After high school, she made plans to attend college locally, but ran out of money after the first semester. From there, she enlisted in a special military intelligence program and soon entered the Green to Gold program, which allowed enlisted soldiers to attend college and become commissioned officers. Soon Melody was finishing the college degree she could not afford before and was commissioned as a finance officer.

Melody recently retired after twenty-three years' service. Her husband Mike, an Army chaplain is still on active duty, serving as the XVIII Airborne Corps Chaplain on Fort Bragg, North Carolina. The couple have three sons.

IN THE BEGINNING

Shortly after I arrived at Schofield Barracks, Hawaii, to work with a finance battalion, I walked out of my office into the hallway and met a very outgoing chaplain from a neighboring battalion. He immediately recognized that I was new, introduced himself, and started giving me tips about the area. He had just gotten back from sailing the inner islands, so he was really on a high. I liked that. We became friends and he encouraged me to become scuba diving certified. Our friendship grew over time and eventually we started dating. We were married in 1995.

Key to our success as a dual military couple was early involvement in the Married Army Couples Program. That is how the Army makes good on its promise to help keep couples together.

I was still in Hawaii but Mike had moved to an assignment in Alaska when we got married. The moment we had our marriage license, we registered with the program. They won't even talk to you before you are married.

We immediately requested "joint domicile" for our next assignments. This means the Army will work to assign the two of you to the same location. But you have to do more than just sign up for the program. You must be really proactive about working with your branch assignment managers. There are a lot of factors the Army assignments people must consider, so you need to give them time to work it out.

In our case, we had two different branches to deal with, Finance Branch and Chaplain Corps. So once we got married we started contacting our branch managers. Even though each of us had about a year left on our assignments, we knew we could not wait until the last minute to arrange our next moves. To make sure there were no problems getting our first assignments in the same spot, Mike and I ended up going to Washington, D.C., to speak with our branch managers face to face. That made a big difference. One year later we were both serving at Fort Jackson, South Carolina.

MAKING A LIVING

CAREERS AND JOINT DOMICILE

Throughout our careers we had a lot of success in working through our assignments together, largely because we decided early on that since Mike was senior in rank to me, his career path would be the one to guide us. You have to choose at the beginning. You really can't flip flop back and forth and say, "Well, we'll take your best assignment this time and mine next time." Some people try to do that, and I don't think that works out well in the end. As soon as the Chaplaincy assigned Mike, we'd start looking for a job for me.

This was especially important when it came to my decision about competing for command. I had to do some real soul-searching. If you want to be in the Army, and if you want to be promoted to full colonel, you need to command a battalion when you are a lieutenant colonel. You have to be willing to go anywhere and take any command they will give you. For me, that would most likely have meant that Mike and I would not be assigned together. I didn't want to pull the family apart and be away from my husband and children. So I made the decision not to be considered for selection as a commander. Three times I declined to go before the selection board.

I'm retiring now as a lieutenant colonel, and it's all good. I don't regret my decision to do it that way.

THE CALENDAR SCRUB

Getting assigned to the same location is just one part of surviving as a dual military couple. When both you and your husband wear the uniform, keeping your schedules straight is very challenging. Some couples make the decision quite early that it is just too hard for both people to stay in because it stretches your family really thin. But Mike was very supportive of my career. He never took the attitude that "you should get out and make sure things are covered at the house." Instead, he said, "We will make this work. We will find a way." So we both kept our military careers, and by the grace of God it all worked out.

> **When both you and your husband wear the uniform, keeping your schedules straight is very challenging.**

How did we do it? We adopted an Army practice called "the calendar scrub." Every week we sat down and discussed what was coming up the next six weeks. Since we spoke the same "Army language," this was pretty easy for us. We would constantly track what he had to do and what I had to do: day by day, week by week, from regular meetings and unit events to field training exercises and deployments.

It was especially challenging around the holidays because we often had conflicting events. Mike would say, "We gotta do the calendar scrub!" and then we would plan it all out. We lived by that calendar.

COMMUNICATION

Keeping the marriage together requires great communication, but that is hard at home with constant interruptions from children, phones, you name it. When Mike and I were working on the same military post, we would go to lunch together every day. This helped a lot because we could discuss what's going on and what's coming up without disturbances. Our ability to communicate and focus on each other this way helped us keep it together through tough situations. I really miss those lunches right now. Currently I work in the city, and he works on a military post, so it is a rare occasion when we get to have lunch together.

FAMILY CARE PLANS

When a dual military couple has children, the Army requires that a valid, workable plan be in place for care of those children in case both parents are deployed. They call this the Family Care Plan. Some families will make one up just to have something in their files to meet the requirements, and then suddenly they get the word to deploy and their plan doesn't work. This can be a disaster for the family and the unit. You have to have a plan that makes sense and that everyone has agreed upon.

We had our Family Care Plan from the time the boys were born, and when they were old enough to understand we made sure they knew the plan.

Mike and I could never have kept both of our careers without the support of family and friends. When the boys were born, we knew we needed to identify that support system. Mike's sister Sheila and brother-in-law Jaime agreed that they would take care of the boys if needed. Over the years, each time we had to update our Family Care Plan, we talked with Sheila and Jaime to reaffirm the agreement. We were so blessed to have that kind of support.

PREPARING THE KIDS FOR DEPLOYMENT

Not only is it important to work through your Family Care Plan with the family or friends who will take care of the children, it is even more important to discuss it with the children themselves! We had our Family

Care Plan from the time the boys were born, and when they were old enough to understand, we made sure they knew the plan. We did a lot to build a very close relationship between the boys and Sheila and Jaime. When we were stationed in the Carolinas, we spent almost every four-day holiday at Sheila's house. If we were stationed anywhere in the States we made it a point to visit eight to ten times a year. As the boys were growing up, they would often hear, "If something happens, you are going to go live with Aunt Sheila and Uncle Jaime." It was a way of life, and so there were no surprises for them when we prepared to deploy.

DEPLOYED TOGETHER

In 2008, the situation we had prepared for came to pass. Mike and I were assigned to Fort Drum, New York, and the 10th Mountain Division had orders to deploy to Iraq. We were both going away for at least a year, and Sheila and Jaime had to make good on their promise to help. So we shipped the boys to their aunt and uncle's farm, and Mike and I shipped to Baghdad.

When we settled in to our camp, we realized Mike needed to be over in the 10th Mountain area and I needed to be by my contracting office, in case of emergency, so it didn't work out for us to share quarters. But we tried to see each other daily. We worked out a routine where we were going to the gym together and having meals together as much as we could. Having him there certainly was great; we could comfort each other when times were tough. But it was still hard on us because we were both missing the children.

KEEPING IN TOUCH WITH THE KIDS

We had to work very hard to stay in touch with the kids while we were in Iraq. Mike did that better than I did. He established a consistent time that he would call, every day. Mike would get up about 4 a.m. (Iraq time), which was just about the time the boys would be going to bed. I think that was good for them, even though it would become hard sometimes because they didn't know what to say. This was especially true for Jonah, who was six, and not that comfortable on the phone yet.

But even though Jonah wasn't big on talking on the phone, it was still important to get that call. He would hear Mike's voice on the phone, same time, every day. This created an important pattern of consistency for him—and for his brothers. The fact that the phone was gonna ring and they knew their Dad was gonna be there made all the difference.

My work schedule did not allow me to be as consistent about calling, but I would still try to call at least five days a week. I generally worked until almost midnight, so I would call from the office at about 10 p.m., which was morning for them. We both sent letters and cards, too. Mike would write a lot. I sent more cards and little gifts. This helped, but it was still really hard being halfway around the world from them.

MANAGING SEPARATION FROM THE CHILDREN

The loss that I felt when separated from my children was so extreme I could not face the entire time all at once. It was just too long, too overwhelming to consider. So I would just pick out the next major event and only focus on that. We got to Baghdad in June, and the first major family event I would miss was Jonah's birthday in September. I would only concentrate on that and not even let my mind think about anything past that time. I talked to Jonah about his birthday party. We planned it. I ordered party supplies online. Because I just dealt with making it to that one thing, it really helped.

After Jonah's birthday, Halloween was the next big event. I focused on that with

Work through deployment separation in manageable chunks; don't try to face the whole thing all at once.

the kids and sent packages. This way I handled the deployment in time chunks, instead of trying to face the whole thing at once. After Halloween, there was Thanksgiving, and, of course, Christmas, and then there was my mid-tour leave.

Work through deployment separation in manageable chunks; don't try to face the whole thing all at once.

WHEN THE MOM DEPLOYS

I did not handle my first deployment as well as I did the one to Iraq.

In 2002 I deployed to Afghanistan. My boys were twelve, eighteen months and nine months old when I left. I was only gone six months, thank God, but it was really, really awful. The hardest thing I have ever had to do in my life was to leave my baby like that. We had a day nanny who came to the house every day to help Mike. It was hard on him; two kinds of diapers, two levels of baby food, Jonah still on the bottle.

Talk to someone. Don't let it eat you up. It was hard talking to my family when I was so far away, but it was much worse for them and for me when we weren't talking.

I was so distraught when I left that I couldn't even think about them, so I didn't even call. I know it was bad, but I couldn't face it.

A month went by, and I still didn't call.

Mike ran into the husband of my boss on Fort Bragg and asked, "Are you hearing anything from Ruthann? Have you heard from her?"

Her husband said, "Yeah, I hear from her quite a bit!"

Word got back to my boss, and she pulled me aside and said, "What is going on, and why aren't you calling your family?"

I just started bawling. I told her I couldn't face it.

If you are having trouble dealing with a separation and you think not talking about it will help, well, it won't. Talk to someone. Don't let it eat you up. It was hard talking to my family when I was so far away, but it was much worse for them and for me when we weren't talking.

THE CHAPLAIN'S WIFE

Before I met Mike, I never could have imagined I would end up married to a chaplain. I was raised Catholic and confirmed Catholic. Mike is Methodist, so when I married him, I became Methodist. I'm good with that, even though there are some things I miss about the Catholic Church. But it's not like I've really given that up. It is still inside me, but I think it is important to support my husband and go to the Methodist church. I figure God is happy that I go somewhere; it doesn't really matter what denomination.

> **When you are married to a chaplain, you have a unique relationship with the unit.**

When you are married to a chaplain, you have a unique relationship with the unit. People view you differently. It is important for the chaplain and the chaplain's spouse to be very involved in the social activities of the chaplain's unit if at all possible.

That has been a challenge for Mike and me because I have been busy with my own career. But to the best of my ability, I tried to support all the social functions or other types of family functions in Mike's units. When he would sponsor retreats, I would try to be there. I did my best to serve as a role model in the unit. It is comforting for the soldiers to see their chaplains and be close to them in a personal kind of way. As the spouse, you become part of the team and inherit some of that.

Sometimes you are unable to fulfill the natural role that everyone expects. You can't do it all. When that happens, it's okay to ask for help.

Traditionally, the spouse of the senior chaplain in a large unit like a division or corps will be the leader for chaplain spouses' meetings. When Mike was the Division Chaplain for 10th Mountain Division, I could not do that because I was deploying. So I handed that responsibility off to another chaplain's wife who was in a better position to do it. She wanted to lead the spouses' group, so that was fine. I attended as many meetings as I could until I deployed. Then I had to let go and know they were in good hands.

MAKING A LIFE

MOVING CHALLENGES

The last five years have been rough for us because we've relocated every year. We moved from Korea to New York, went into Iraq, came back went to Fort Bragg, then to Fort Knox, and now we are going back to Fort Bragg.

It's always a pretty huge challenge for us to move because we are both working full time. When we arrive at a new location, we get the house somewhat set up, just to get it functional. It takes time because we can only do one or two boxes a night. So if we move in the summer, we may not feel like we have our lives back in order until Thanksgiving!

> That's a linchpin in the move—getting your new place locked in ahead of time.

When families are moving, it is important to line up housing prior to arriving at the new location, if at all possible. This takes a huge amount of stress off you. Otherwise, you are living in temporary housing, possibly for months, while you look for permanent housing. If you can have your new place already lined up, then you are way ahead of the game. That's a linchpin in the move—getting your new place locked in ahead of time.

When Mike and I were not able to get that done, it proved to be a terrible strain on the family. During the last three moves, we were in limbo for months while we waited to get housing. One time we were told we would have housing on post, but would have to stay in temporary housing about a month for it to be ready. So we put the kids in school on base since that was where we would be living. We went back thirty days later only to be told they no longer were going to have a house for us. That was difficult, to say the least! There was a housing crunch, and we couldn't find anything to rent near post, but we were not going to switch our kids to a different school. We just couldn't do that to them again. So we ended up driving our kids to school every day for the next year.

This is why, given a choice, I would not live on post. I don't ever want to set myself up for that again. Hopefully, now that I am retired and can spend more time planning the move, we'll never move without having someplace lined up to live. That's my goal.

CHILDREN AND MOVES

When children are little, they move pretty easily, but moving can become difficult as they get older. With Alex we were lucky because we were able to stay in Korea long enough for him to finish high school. We had moved between his freshman and sophomore years, but after that we were able to keep him in the same school until he graduated.

Now Jacob and Jonah are reaching that stage. Our move back to North Carolina is hugely positive for them because it's a place where they have been before. They were not as happy to come to Kentucky, so we had to work ahead to prepare them. We usually do research about the new place and start to let the kids know what interesting things are there. We make plans for trips and family outings and get them involved.

For a while we thought we were going out to Washington State, and the boys were bummed because they were hoping to go back to North

Carolina. So we talked about it and said, "Now wait, there are a lot of really neat things on the West Coast that we might get to do." We started to research it online, and talked about possible trips to the Grand Canyon, Mount Rushmore, and even Alaska. We tried to open their eyes to what's available at the assignment and focus on that. In the end, it turned out we were going back to North Carolina, but they were ready for Washington if that came through.

SPONSORSHIP PROGRAM

When a new family comes into the Army, the Total Army Sponsorship Program is really important. It can make or break you early on. A sponsor is someone from your new unit selected to help you get settled in. A good sponsor will really be there for you, show you the community and help you find a place to live. You will rely heavily on that sponsor. If your sponsor for some reason doesn't seem to be fulfilling that role, then look for another mentor who has been around awhile and knows the area.

For an Army family, the chapel is not a bad place to start looking. There are a number of women's groups whose members are happy to help explain the ropes. But if your family does not typically go to church, there are other organizations there for you.

Check out Army Community Service (ACS) and the ACS's Army Family Team Building classes. They're really good, and they usually offer childcare. They have various levels of classes, teaching beginners how to read a Leave and Earnings Statement (LES) and what to do with TRICARE (your medical insurance) while helping more advanced students manage deployments or learn to lead others.

COMMITMENT TO SERVICE

When a woman marries a soldier or her husband joins the military, she probably has no way of knowing just how much sacrifice is going to be required. If I had a close friend who was marrying a soldier, I would explain that it is going to be a huge sacrifice but also hugely rewarding. The Army has to be a good fit for both spouses. If one loves the Army and the other hates it, it's not going to work out well.

When the reality hits, the Army wife has to take to it and say, "This is it, this is what our family does, and we're committed to this. We're going to absorb the pain."

There will be the pain of separations, the pain of the moves. You have to do it because that's what you want to do; you are committed to your service. If a spouse

When a woman marries a soldier or her husband joins the military, she probably has no way of knowing just how much sacrifice is going to be required.

isn't all that patriotic or doesn't feel acknowledged for the sacrifices she is making, it won't work.

There are plenty of families that say, "this is just too much, we're gonna get out." I don't blame them for that. That's an individual decision. It's your family, your children. Each family has to decide how to respond.

DUAL MILITARY COUPLES UNDERSTAND THE PRESSURES

When you are part of a dual military couple, it is easier to understand the pressures on each other. For example, when I was a company commander and I was working six-and-a-half days a week—in all day on Saturday and still training a half day on Sunday—some couples would have argued over this schedule, but Mike was very supportive.

He never ever said, "What are you doing? Why aren't you spending time with the family?" Instead, he understood what I was going through. And I did the same for him.

When he had to leave in the middle of the night for whatever kind of emergency or he had to work the weekend, I would understand. It's just the way it is. We didn't have as many issues of feeling rejected or left out or undervalued because we both knew this is just part of what the Army demands. Dual military has been a very, very positive thing for Mike and me. We both love it because we really love the Army.

The hardest thing about my decision to retire is that the Army has been my whole identity. I managed to stay in for a full career, and it was great. I'm glad Mike and I hung in and I got to finish out the career, but it's time to do something else. I don't even know what I'm gonna do next, but that's okay. I am praying on it.

BECKY APEL

"The year of my husband's deployment was very empowering for me."

A native of Seattle, Washington, Becky moved to Wasilla, Alaska, with her family when she was a senior in high school, and has called Alaska home for thirty years. She met Rob Apel, an Alaska National Guard soldier, while they were both working at a fast-food restaurant. Becky was nineteen and Rob was in his twenties when they fell in love. They've now been married more than twenty-five years and have a grown son and daughter.

MAKING A LIVING

TIME AWAY

When I met Rob, his Army schedule was easy to understand. He was a traditional Army Guard soldier attending one weekend drill per month, plus one two-week annual training event per year. Got it.

However, I didn't know there would also be large chunks of time that he'd have to spend away in school. Soldiers have all sorts of training they must attend if they want to be promoted to the next rank. Just about the time we got married, Rob was selected for the Active Guard Reserve (AGR) program. These soldiers serve full time supporting a National Guard or Army Reserve unit. They receive the same benefits as active duty soldiers.

Pressure is really on for AGR soldiers to attend all required schooling. The Primary Leadership Development Course (PLDC), the Basic Non-Commissioned Officer Course (BNCOC) and Advanced Non-Commissioned Officer Course (ANCOC) prepared enlisted soldiers to serve at the next higher rank. (These courses are now called Warrior Leader Course, Advanced Leader Course, and Senior Leader Course.) Between PLDC, BNCOC and ANCOC, Rob would be away for weeks and weeks at a time. This was especially tough when the kids were little. I was young, and I wasn't expecting the time pressures the Army would place on Rob. He is a very dedicated person, a very dedicated soldier, so he was often working late nights and that kind of thing. He was a master sergeant for many years. Now he is the first sergeant of a military police company—the highest ranking noncommissioned officer in the company—which means he did a pretty good job all those years taking care of his unit and getting all the training he needed.

I really didn't know what I was getting into when we were married. Be prepared. If your husband is in the National Guard and wants to progress, he will have to do more than just the monthly drill weekends. Sometimes your husband may have to be away for weeks at a time, and that's not counting deployments.

DEPLOYMENT

My husband deployed with fifteen other men from the Alaska National Guard in September 2008. They were an Embedded Transition Team (ETT) serving in Afghanistan. He was gone for a whole year.

When he was getting ready to leave, Rob asked me if I wanted to be the Family Readiness Group (FRG) leader. I said, "Not really," because I didn't know what that meant. But he kept asking me. There wasn't anyone else to do it, and since I wasn't working at the time, I was the best choice.

Finally I said, "Look, to support you and the other men, I will go in and see what would be involved."

I visited the local Army Family Assistance Center (FAC) and talked to the Family Readiness Support Assistant, who was there to provide support for FRG leaders.

She explained that sometimes when small groups of sixteen deploy (like ours), they don't get the same kind of attention as the groups that are one hundred soldiers or more. Some of our soldiers had mentioned to her that they did not want to be forgotten.

WHAT A FAMILY READINESS GROUP DOES

- Serve as a liaison organization between the command and families
- Make sure soldiers are not forgotten
- Bring families together for meetings
- Organize the sending of care packages
- Help supply resources to the families of deployed soldiers in need

I knew right then I needed to do this. I didn't want our guys to be forgotten either. So I volunteered to be the FRG leader, to bring the families together for meetings, send care packages, and stuff like that.

Volunteering to be the FRG leader was the best thing I could have done for my family. I myself had no idea what kinds of resources were available until I visited the regional Family Assistance Center. These centers were set up in response to the high number of deployments, for all the families needing help.

The Family Readiness Support Assistant explained that part of her job is serving as a liaison between the command and families. The Family Assistance Center calls the families of the deployed service members once a month just to check on them. They find out if the family needs anything and then help supply resources. As I said, I didn't even know all this help existed.

GETTING PAST DEPLOYMENT SHOCK

Rob's deployment to Afghanistan came as a real shock. He had been in the Guard for years and never deployed overseas. Way back when Desert Storm started, I was nervous that he might deploy. He told me not to worry about it because National Guard soldiers were more likely to go somewhere in Alaska or to another state to help out with natural disasters or something similar. Right after 9/11 there seemed to be a lot of units deploying, and we started thinking that he might have to go. But the wars in Afghanistan and Iraq went on for years and he didn't deploy. Then, suddenly, we got the news that he was deploying.

Here is what you go through when you get the news your husband will deploy: First, you are in shock. You don't believe it. Then you start to think of all the stuff you have to get done before he goes, and you start running around to do it all. And then, wow, it's here and your husband goes away. It can all be pretty draining.

My daughter was nineteen at the time, just about ready to move out on her own. But she waited until her dad returned from deployment, and it was nice that she stuck around. She was old enough to give me support, and I didn't have to worry about her.

I was very fortunate that my kids were older; I don't think I could have made it through so well with little kids. Originally I considered telling my daughter to go ahead and move out, but I'm glad I didn't. Having family with me made the separation easier.

DON'T BURDEN HIM WITH THE LITTLE PROBLEMS HE CAN'T FIX

While Rob was away from home, I tried very hard to follow one piece of advice a friend gave me. She pointed out that Rob is my "go-to" guy. When things go wrong, I go to him for help. She said after he leaves, when things go wrong (the sink breaks, car trouble), don't bog him down with it. Even during their pre-deployment training at Fort Riley, Kansas, my friend told me not to burden him with stuff that needs to be fixed. It will be on his mind, distract him from what he is doing, and he can't do anything about it anyway!

> When things go wrong . . . [don't] burden him with stuff that needs to be fixed. It will be on his mind, distract him from what he is doing, and he can't do anything about it anyway!

This was extremely difficult for me. When he would call on the phone, I wanted to tell him about all the things that were broke or going wrong. But I didn't. I stuck to it and didn't talk about anything negative. I didn't burden him with things he couldn't do anything about.

Funny thing is, while he was still in Kansas, the sink really did break! I had seen him take some little thing off, unclog it and screw it back on. So I said, "I can do this!" I did everything just right, but it still leaked. So I placed a big bowl underneath the sink and contacted a plumber from our church who easily fixed it. I discovered I really could take care of it without bothering Rob!

> **Looking back, the year of my husband's deployment was very empowering for me.**

One day afterward, I happened to mention to Rob, "Oh yeah, the sink had a bad leak, but it's fixed so don't worry about it!"

He said, "Why didn't you tell me? Why didn't you phone me about it?"

"Well honey," I said, "What were you going to do about it? You couldn't fix it."

You know, there was nothing he really could say.

Looking back, the year of my husband's deployment was very empowering for me. I learned that I could take care of myself if I really needed to. I did a lot of stuff that Rob normally did for both of us. I drove a little tractor to pile the snow out of the driveway. Things like that. But believe me, I was more than happy to give those chores back to him when he returned!

DEPLOYMENT COMMUNICATION: PHONE CALLS CAN BE NUTS

How we communicated during the deployment depended on where Rob was in Afghanistan. The first half of the year we were able to Skype a couple times a week or more. The second half we couldn't Skype. He was in a different location and his computer access wasn't great. We did email, and sometimes we would chat on the computer. And of course, I sent care packages.

Phone calls were nuts. It was frustrating because we would get only five or ten minutes into a phone call and get cut off. It was nice hearing his voice, but we found ourselves rushing to say goodbye. We hated to be cut off in the middle of a conversation.

Just because another soldier's spouse says they talk each night on Skype or on the phone, don't assume you will have the same opportunity. Every location is different. Sometimes the Army builds a new base, and when the soldiers first move in they have no Internet or phone access. Another base only ten miles away might have cable, Internet, everything.

RETURNING HOME: EVERYTHING IS SUBJECT TO CHANGE WITHOUT NOTICE

I had been told that when your soldier returns home from deployment, you don't have to tell him everything the first day. I tried not to overwhelm Rob with everything that had been going on while he was gone, but I couldn't help it. I just kept talking and talking and talking. I think I probably wore him out with all that talking.

We took a special three-week trip up the coast of California after he came back from Afghanistan, but we didn't finalize any of the plans until he was home. It is dangerous to plan too much ahead of time, assuming the unit will be back on a specific date. It rarely works out that way.

But some people don't understand that. They buy plane tickets, make special plans

When your soldier returns home from deployment, you don't have to tell him everything the first day.

and then have to change them. When the team was training in Kansas, just before deploying for Afghanistan, there was talk that they might be able to come back home for Thanksgiving before they left. But there is always talk about this or that! They *were* going to have three weeks leave, then they *weren't* gonna get any leave, then we heard they would have a week. Some of the guys bought tickets because they heard they were maybe coming home. They had to keep rescheduling them.

All the back and forth made me really frustrated. Then Rich, from the Family Assistance Center, reminded me of something that I know my husband had told me countless times: "In the Army everything is subject to change without notice." He kept pounding that into my brain through the whole deployment. I probably still had expectations, but in the end I could say, "You're right, he could come home any time. It's all subject to change."

> **In the Army everything is subject to change without notice.**

Rob ended up only having three days at the beginning of November. He did not come home, but I was able to fly down to Kansas to see him.

MAKING A LIFE

ARMY NATIONAL GUARD CHALLENGES

Active duty soldiers usually live on or near a military post with other military families as neighbors to support them when there is a deployment. On the other hand, traditional Army National Guard soldiers live in the civilian community and basically have two jobs: their civilian job and their once-a-month duties as a soldier. They don't have all the same military resources available right where they are and have to rely on the civilian community for support.

This is especially true in a state like Alaska. People are dispersed over a very large area. Some of our villages can't even be reached by car. Soldiers from these communities actually have to fly to their weekend drill locations. In these villages, families need to rely on the Native Council for support. If a soldier belongs to an Alaska Native Tribe, he may be one of the community's subsistence providers, hunting to bring in meat that will help feed the community through the winter. If that soldier is deployed for a year, the council has to work out a plan to help feed families in his absence.

The entire community must be involved to ensure families are supported during deployments. I know a woman who had to stay home from work to help prepare the seals her husband had caught. The meat and skins from those seals would provide for the family while he was deployed. We don't realize how important each individual is to the Alaska Native community. Everyone has a role. It is a big sacrifice when they send someone away to the Army. The military works with the council and doesn't demand that a specific man leave for a deployment. The Native Council decides who that will be. And then the family whose soldier deploys must rely on the rest of the community for assistance.

> [Reservists] don't have all the same military resources available right where they are and have to rely on the civilian community for support.

ACRONYMS

It seems like everything the Army talks about, all the words they make up, get put into acronyms. If you want to understand what your husband is talking about when he comes home, then learn what some of the more common acronyms mean. This will help you avoid some misunderstandings. I haven't been very successful, but I keep trying.

You don't have to learn everything and be like a big encyclopedia. No one expects you to have a PhD in Army, but your husband will notice and appreciate it if you can follow his conversation.

POLITICS

The Army can be very political. I didn't understand this at first. A commander will say, "We are having a banquet and it is highly recommended that you attend." Basically, that means you really *must* attend. They won't order your husband to go, but they will remember it if he doesn't, and it will hurt him later.

It always seemed a little silly to me. Rob would come home and say, "Well, I've got to attend this ceremony."

"We've gotta do that??" I'd say.

Then I started to realize we don't *have* to do it, but we *should* do it. I began to tolerate those kinds of events because it made a difference for him. Even now, it still seems silly, and sometimes costs a lot of money, but I suck it up and do it to support Rob.

UNREALISTIC EXPECTATIONS

I wasn't too involved with unit activities early in our marriage. There was no real threat of deployment, and his National Guard work was like any other job. I didn't feel the need to understand what he did or worry about what might happen to him.

There was a flood in Talkeetna, and he was activated to go support recovery efforts. No big deal; he was only gone a short while. I knew it was military, but it was different. Then suddenly he was going to deploy, and that changed everything. He was going to be away much longer, in a dangerous place. It was a whole different thing, a whole different life.

It is important to recognize that National Guard soldiers live two different lives. There are times when the governor says, "We need you," and they go help with disaster response. And then there are the times when the president says, "We need you," and they go somewhere in the world to a combat zone. I wasn't ready for the second one.

The year he was gone was really tough. But in the end, I'm glad he did it. Rob loves what he does. He is very dedicated to his soldiers and to his country. I am extremely proud of him.

DANIELLE SHELL

"Arm yourself with all kinds of knowledge."

R aised an Army brat, Danielle Shell thought that she knew everything she needed to know about the military—until she became an Army wife. Things changed after the attacks of 9/11, and the United States would be at war for over ten years. She already understood being strong and steadfast and taking deployment in stride.

What no one could teach her, however, was how to deal with the pain of a spouse being severely injured in combat. But Danielle learned quickly, and shares the wisdom that has come from experience. Her husband, Alvin, was a captain when he medically retired in 2006. He was with the 21st MP Company, 16th MP Brigade (ABN).

IN THE BEGINNING

I was born a twin in Salisbury, Maryland, to a teen mom. We moved to Philadelphia to be near my mom's parents. We didn't have much money, and lived off food stamps, government cheese—the whole deal. My mom made the decision to join the Army to provide a better life for my sister and me when we were six years old. She left us in the care of my grandparents. My grandfather taught me what to expect in a husband, father and provider, and was also a stickler for proper manners and table etiquette. My grandmother sparked my love of cooking and gave us unconditional love.

When we were ten, my mom came back for us, along with a new husband. He was an amazing dad and very family-oriented. Thus, we became Army brats and lived in Fort Sill, Oklahoma; Augsburg, Germany (where my little brother was born); Fort Campbell, Kentucky; and Fort Lee, Virginia. Military life taught me how to be personable and to accept change at any given moment with grace. My mother taught me how to be strong and focused—she had to be able to juggle being a mother, wife and soldier. She hosted dinner parties and was an Air Assault Senior Noncommissioned Officer. Because of the Army, I got to meet so many different people and experience such a mix of cultures that I now try to accept people for who they are and not be judgmental of

Arm yourself with all kinds of knowledge! You can never know too much—but you can certainly get into trouble by knowing too little.

those who have faiths, beliefs and lifestyles that are different from my own.

I met Alvin in 1996, when we were both in college and working at Red Lobster. We hit it off immediately. Alvin and I were married on July 3, 1999, at the Fort Lee Chapel.

MAKING A LIVING

Alvin's joining the Army was originally my idea, but he soon agreed. He had been working in corrections after graduating college and had so much potential. Having seen officers and noncommissioned officers in the Army for most of my life, I knew that he had what it would take to be successful. I wasn't wrong—it fit him so well.

Soon our sons Alvin III (Trey) and Jachin arrived as younger brothers for Sean. We have had our struggles along the way, but each struggle makes us stronger. I know we are setting a great example of love, strength and commitment for our children.

Nothing is worse than your telling too much personal information about your husband to the people with whom he works.

KNOWLEDGE IS KEY

Arm yourself with all kinds of knowledge! You can never know too much—but you can certainly get into trouble by knowing too little.

There are many resources available for the asking. The Army Community Service (ACS) and Family Advocacy Program (FAP) are great assets for newcomers. Take advantage of them.

Talk to other spouses, especially the ones who have been in for a while. They have an endless supply of knowledge. Be careful, though; nothing is worse than your telling too much personal information about your husband to the people with whom he works. Don't spread your family business around. That is when gossip starts and that is not a good thing!

Try not to partake in gossip; it's not healthy and it will only bite you later on. Trust me on this.

ASK QUESTIONS

I spent numerous hours at the ACS in Germany brushing up on my Army lingo and chain of command structures—even after growing up Army—and boy, was it helpful.

> **You have to be okay with being a single parent when necessary and not blame your husband for it.**

I also volunteered with FAP and became the Family Readiness Group (FRG) leader while in Germany. This is pretty uncommon when you're the spouse of a Specialist SPC (E-4). I made a point of talking to each person individually and getting to know them personally. As a result I met some really wonderful people in the unit. I don't know what I would have done without the help of the other spouses. Just talking to women who were in the same boat as me was invaluable. Even though I knew what it was like to be an Army child, I still needed to learn to be an Army spouse.

Between your husband's constant deployments and all his training, your life can get very lonely, very fast. Arm yourself with your own friends, hobbies and passions. If you expect your spouse to give you everything that you need, you'll be miserable. You have to be okay with being a single parent when necessary and not blame your husband for it. As quickly as possible, learn to just roll with the punches!

DEPLOYMENTS

When your husband is deployed, make sure you keep yourself busy. If that means getting a job, going home to stay with family, or going back to school, then do it.

Whatever you do, stay in contact with someone from the unit Rear Detatchment (Rear D) or the FRG. Seeing something on the CNN ticker and not having a way to find out if it affects your spouse while in country is unnerving to say the least.

Keep your contacts close!

BE PREPARED TO DROP EVERYTHING AND GO

Always have a current passport.

When your husband is deployed, make sure you keep yourself busy. If that means getting a job, going home to stay with family, or going back to school, then do it.

I'll never forget Tuesday, August 31, 2004; I was folding clothes in my bedroom when the phone rang. On the line was Captain Mike Eby, my husband's commander. I knew that whatever he was about to say could not be good—commanders never call just to say hello.

He told me as gently as possible that Alvin had been hurt. He'd been in a roadside attack and was on his way to the Landstuhl Regional Medical Center in Ramstein, Germany. Captain Eby provided me with so much information at one time that it took me a while to process it. After hanging up, I took a breath and started to analyze what I needed to do.

I knew at some point I would have to leave my boys to go to wherever Alvin was. I decided not to say too much to them until I had all the facts.

Later Colonel Dave Quantock, the Brigade Commander for Alvin's unit, called me back. He gave me exactly what I needed—the real details and not a cushioned answer. I prefer it that way. Don't candy-coat it. Give it to me straight.

Have phone numbers and legal documents in a safe and easily accessible place. Make sure to have a passport in case of emergencies.

He told me that Alvin was out on patrol, responding to a downed vehicle when a rocket propelled grenade (RPG) was fired at the soldiers, causing an explosion that surrounded them in flames. He said that Alvin was a hero because he ran through the wall of fire to save a fellow soldier. In doing so, Alvin caught fire and was badly burned. Colonel Quantock told me to be prepared in case it played out in such a way that I would want to go to Germany to be with my husband (this is when that passport is a necessity!).

The best thing that Colonel Quantock did for me that day was to let me speak to the doctor who had just operated on Alvin. The surgeon told me the extent of his injuries and what I would probably have to deal with in the near future.

As things progressed, it turned out I didn't need to go to Germany after all. Instead Alvin was placed in a medically induced coma and sent to the Fort Sam Houston Burn Center in Texas.

My mom was a huge support. Without her I wouldn't have stayed as focused as I did. A sister's love cannot be measured; my sister, without question, was the one person who listened and let me vent. You are not good to anyone if you lose control or break down!

Alvin's mom took it very hard, and that was expected because no mother wants to hear about her child being hurt. All I could do was let her know I was there for her. His father was a rock, as always. He traveled to Texas to be with Alvin and me.

My dad called and told me that he was coming down to stay with the boys for as long as I needed him. That was amazing to me—he dropped *everything* and came to take care of my boys. This is where family is important!

There was also an outpouring of support from the officers' wives and from our friends. I don't think that (now) Major Michael Eby, (now) General Dave and Melissa Quantock and my family even realize how their support in those first days shaped how well the next two years of rehab and surgeries would go.

Remember it's important to be prepared for anything in the military. Have phone numbers and legal documents in a safe and easily accessible place. Make sure to have a passport in case of emergencies. The passport is usually a happy thing—you'll need it when your soldier goes on R&R. With any luck, you'll get to travel to an interesting meeting point.

MAKING A LIFE

MOVING
The secret to handling a move is **ORGANIZATION!**

- When you know a move is on the horizon, start planning *before you get the orders.* Begin to eliminate things you don't need, have grown out of or just plain have too many of. Donating unneeded goods to a veteran's organization is a perfect way to clean house while helping others. If you have children, there's no need to move clothes or shoes they've outgrown. You can always acquire new, more current things when you get to your new location. The less you take the easier it will be. It's hard enough to corral the kids, let alone a hundred boxes.

• Buy colored markers and labels. Each room and child gets assigned a color. Before any box leaves the old house, it should be color-coded on all sides.

• Think about what you will need when you arrive at the new location in the days before the moving van does. Box those things up and put them in your car. Include entertainment for the kids: movies, games and coloring books to keep them busy. You will also need cooking utensils, bedding, clothes for a week, an iron and ironing board, and curtains to cover the bare windows of your new place.

• At the new home, identify the rooms with the coordinating color before the movers arrive. That way, as the boxes come in, everyone knows which room each box belongs in. The movers can do most of the work without asking. No need to stand there and read the writing on every box that comes through the door. Don't get me wrong; there are still stray boxes, but only one or two versus ten to fifteen. The kids get to help, and unpacking is way easier when everything is in the correct room.

• The faster you can get the home in order, the easier it will be for your spouse to focus on his mission and do his new job.

I always felt that I was his support system; if I didn't do my job well, he couldn't do his.

- If there's something you don't know, find out! You can't be timid and be an effective military spouse. Perhaps that's sad—but very, very true.

BECOME ACCLIMATED TO YOUR NEW NEIGHBORHOOD

Educate yourself about your new surroundings as soon as possible. I begin to get my bearings by finding out where the nearest stores are. This way I know how to get the necessities for my family even if my husband is busy at work. Walk the neighborhood, study a map of the area and take a drive. Scouting is one of the jobs that we Army spouses do well.

BEING A TEAM

Make sure that you have strong family ties while in the military. Army life can be tough. If the love and commitment between spouses are not strong enough, it can break you. It's important to communicate with your spouse about how you are feeling. Don't be afraid to be truthful with each other, because this has to be a team effort!

Communicate with your husband. Understand that a lot of the things your soldier has to do are not his choice. He can't tell his commanding officer that he can't go to the field because his wife doesn't

MOVING

- The secret is organization
- Start planning before you get the orders.
- Eliminate things you have grown out of or just plain have too many of.
- Donate unneeded goods to a veteran's organization.
- The less you take the easier it will be.
- Each room and child gets assigned a color–color code each box on all sides.
- Box things you will need when you arrive at your new location and put them in your car.
- The faster you get the home in order, the easier it will be for your spouse to focus on his mission.

> **Understand that a lot of the things your soldier has to do are not his choice. He can't tell his commanding officer that he can't go to the field because his wife doesn't want him to.**

want him to. You have to understand and be willing to give up a fair amount of control. As a spouse, you need to smoothly roll past the bumps that this life brings because at some point they will come!

BRINGING US CLOSER

I truly feel like Alvin's accident brought our family closer together. Having him come so close to death has taught us never to take each other for granted, to really appreciate the time that we do have, and to keep the ones that we love close.

It's important to remember that tomorrow is not promised to anyone, so relish the time with your loved ones daily!

Alvin and I now make date nights, and he takes off to do things with our boys. At the time of the accident, he was on the fast track. Alvin was supposed to leave Iraq, then turn around and go right back with the 82d Airborne Division. Work came first. Not anymore. It's important for military couples to make the effort to stay connected. Everything else is just background noise. When your spouse gets back from a deployment, spend at least one day with just the kids. They need that time with dad and they need to get used to family being back as one unit.

> **It's important for military couples to make the effort to stay connected. Everything else is just background noise.**

HELP OF ALL KINDS

Military OneSource is a free service provided by the Department of Defense to service members and their families. It helps with a broad range of concerns including money management, spouse employment and education, parenting and child care, relocation, deployment, reunion, and the particular concerns of families with special-needs members. They can also include more complex issues like sustaining relationships, coping with stress, and grief processes. Military OneSource services are available twenty-four hours a day—by telephone and online.

Help is also available from the Army Community Service, the Family Readiness Group, the Family Advocacy Program, and the base chaplain.

And remember that your family is always a great sounding board when you just need to vent!

JULIE ACEVES

"It took sheer determination not to give up."

Born in Lexington, Kentucky, the daughter of a photographer, Julie has been married twice, each time to a soldier. She and her first husband came to Fort Bragg, North Carolina, when she was just sixteen years old. The marriage ended after he became abusive.

Her second (current) husband was a Cavalry Scout, who retired from active duty in January 2010 after his last assignment at Fort Knox, Kentucky. She has over twenty-one years of experience with the Army community.

MAKING A LIVING

ORGANIZE YOUR DOCUMENTS

When I married Dan, he was already in the Army. As I went from office to office getting registered, processed and all that stuff, my marriage license was like gold. I had to have it constantly. Not only that, I had to carry proof of my earlier divorce with me as well. If you have remarried after a divorce, you need to have both your proof of divorce and marriage certificate for most things.

Whether you are just entering the military, or moving, or preparing for your husband's deployment, you've gotta be organized. Keep important paperwork handy. Don't let the packers put it in a box!

MOVING IS THE PITS

Our early moves in the Army were chaos. When my first husband and I arrived at Fort Bragg, North Carolina, we had no idea that there was a waiting list for on-post housing—and the wait was two years! We were suddenly scrambling to find a place to live off post. It was horrible!

Thus, I learned the hard way: always check with the housing office at your new post before arriving. Find out how long you might have to wait to get a house on post. If it will be a long time, then start doing research about the best places to live off post.

My husband achieved the rank of staff sergeant before he retired in 2010. During his career we moved eighteen times. After so many moves I finally accepted that you never do settle in. You shouldn't try to totally settle in. You don't have to unpack everything. Dan and I had a lot of stuff, but most of the time we didn't unpack it all. We considered the space, the location, and said, "Okay, we don't need this here" and then left it in the box.

One of the things we learned early was that things get broken in a move. As long as you are in the military and moving all the time, don't buy anything that you don't want broken. It's gonna get destroyed. Buy the cheap stuff until you get out or until right before you get out.

Of course, you will probably have some fragile things. We started putting our fragile stuff, the stuff we wanted packed really well, in a separate room. When the packers would go to that room, one of us would be there and watch over them. "Pack this really, really well, because it will break," we would say. We would stay on them, and make them redo anything they didn't pack right.

When the movers come to pack your things, it can get really crazy. You definitely need more than one person in the house. Have three or four if you can. Invite some friends over. Have a moving party!

GETTING THROUGH DEPLOYMENTS

It takes a special breed of person to be a military spouse. When your husband is gone, you have to be fiercely independent and do everything on your own. You have to be strong willed and learn how to be alone.

But when your husband returns from deployment, the two of you need to return to being interdependent. I have seen many soldiers come home from deployments and say, "I have nothing to do! I don't know what to do!"

This is because the wife is so caught up running things: "I got it, I got it, I got it," she says. He watches and wonders, "Where do I fit in?" You have to learn that fine art, that fine balance, between independence and interdependence.

> You have to learn that fine art, that fine balance, between independence and interdependence.

And, most of all, you must have patience.

My first husband didn't have any deployments, but he was gone on field exercises a lot. I had to figure out how to be alone for a week. I drove my family and my friends nuts calling them and talking to them for hours.

When my current husband went to Bosnia, it was really hard because they didn't have all the communication technology available today. Later, when he was in Iraq, we had cable and the Internet. We Skyped, we did instant messaging. It was a lot easier.

But during Bosnia I would send a letter and wait and wonder *did he get it yet?* Three weeks later, I'd finally get a letter back answering the one I sent.

During his deployment to Bosnia, I would write down what I did every day: "Today I went to work, and here is what happened at work." I would mail that to him with my letters. It felt stupid, but I think he appreciated it. When he came back on leave, he knew everybody I was talking about, and I didn't have to catch him up on who was who or who did what. I didn't have to pull him aside and say, "Now this person is so and so . . ." He already knew.

MAKING A LIFE

MOVING OVERSEAS WITH CHILDREN

My favorite assignment was Germany. I loved Germany, the country, the people. I loved the lifestyle. But getting the paperwork done for my children took forever. If you have a child with any sort of special medical need, even something as straightforward as asthma, you have to be sure the location where you are being assigned has the right facilities to handle it. The Army labels family members with special needs as "EFMP," which stands for "Exceptional Family Member Program."

My son Christian had been diagnosed with ADD and ADHD, and we planned to take him with us to Germany. Dan was already in Germany, and the kids were with me in Lexington, Kentucky. So I had to drive back and forth to Fort Knox to have Christian evaluated and make sure the diagnoses were correct.

They handed me a questionnaire that must have been fifty sheets long. I was told to fill it out and turn it in. They told me it would take four to six months to process because it had to be signed by several people in different offices.

Four to six months?

When something like that happens, don't accept that it's impossible to make it work. Use your creativity to figure out how to get what they need in a time frame that works for you.

Get the paperwork done early. The minute you find out your husband's next assignment, check to see if there are any limitations regarding family medical issues. They may have to change the assignment.

I discovered that if I walked the papers through myself, getting signatures and taking the paperwork to the next office, things would go much more quickly. So I did it. Instead of taking six months, it took about two and a half months.

On the other hand, a friend of ours moved to Germany without completing all the paperwork. The family arrived at their new location and discovered the local medical community did not have the ability to treat her son's asthma. The husband had to be reassigned to another location in Germany. It was a real mess, and took almost a year to work it out.

Get the paperwork done early. The minute you find out your husband's next assignment, check to see if there are any limitations regarding family medical issues. If it turns out there is a problem, they may have to change the assignment.

WHEN YOUR HUSBAND IS WOUNDED

One of the things that I have told different people over the years is, "If my husband is killed or he is wounded, don't send the military to my door. I don't want that, because it's completely likely I'm gonna hurt somebody." I'm a good ole country girl, and I have a temper. If you throw something like that at me when I am not expecting it, the temper usually comes out!

One day while Dan was deployed to Iraq, I took the kids to the water park. At the end of the day, I came out to the car, checked the phone, and saw that my mother had called me.

When I reached her, she said, "Dan is trying to get ahold of you. He said he would call you back later." It was his birthday, so it seemed normal for him to contact me, but her voice didn't sound quite right when she gave me the message.

We packed up and went right home. I walked in the door and found twelve voicemails from Dan. I thought, "What the hell?" While I was listening to this series of phone messages, which became more and more frantic with each successive call, the phone beeped. It was him in person.

"Happy birthday!" was the first thing out of my mouth.

"Yeah," he said in a funny tone.

IF YOUR SOLDIER IS WOUNDED

- When something bad happens, don't assume all the initial facts that come in are correct.
- If soldiers show up at your door in regular uniforms, don't freak out.
- Ask questions. Do some research. Know your options.
- Get the current phone numbers for Landstuhl Regional Medical Center in Germany where soldiers are sent first on overseas deployments.
- Have all of your important documents and contact information handy.
- Have a support system ("Battle Buddy") in place.

"You sound sick. You sound like you got a cold. You okay?"

"Well, I kinda got a little bit shot."

Of course, the first thing that went through my head was, "Getting a little bit shot is like being a little bit pregnant!"

"What happened, did it just go right through you? Are you okay?"

"I got shot in the arm. I just got out of surgery a little while ago. I'm okay. But they're going to send me home."

He told me they would send him to the hospital in Germany before they sent him back home.

No sooner had I hung up than the company commander called.

"Well," he hesitated. "I got some information for you."

"I know," I said. "My husband's been shot."

He was relieved that I already knew. As it turned out, the information he had was completely wrong. So I was updating him! All he had was the first report that came from the unit overseas.

When something bad happens, don't assume all the initial facts that come in are correct. The first report is not always accurate. Make sure they verify everything. I had the news straight from the horse's mouth, so I had the right scoop.

When something bad happens, don't assume all the initial facts that come in are correct.

As the Captain and I continued talking, he sheepishly admitted that there were two of his soldiers in the neighborhood trying to reach me to notify me about Dan's injury. (He knew how I felt about military coming to my door and surprising me with bad news.) They were in ACUs— army combat uniforms, standard work clothes—rather than their dress uniforms, so I wouldn't assume they were coming to notify me that my husband was dead.

Even with those precautions, all I could think was "Thank you, God, it was Dan who told me." I had heard my husband's voice, so I knew he was alive and conscious.

After I got off the phone with the captain, I had a few minutes to gather myself before they arrived. I thought, "Oh my God, if they had shown up at my door and I hadn't talked to my husband, I would have freaked out!"

So this is something I try to tell friends whose husbands are deploying: "If soldiers show up at your door in *regular uniforms,* don't freak out! He's fine, he's fine, he's fine!"

As it turned out, Dan was not in tip-top condition. Hubby did sugarcoat his injury. I got the full story after he returned home. When he got shot, he was holding his rifle up. The bullet came right down the length of his rifle, and went in between his two middle fingers. It came out his hand, went back in his wrist, and then went into his upper arm and shattered his upper arm completely. It messed him up bad.

MAKE A CLOSE FRIEND

It's very important to find someone, preferably another military wife, who will stick with you when the going gets tough. Soldiers call this person a "battle buddy." It doesn't have to be a military wife, but I think that is better, because she'll know the system. She'll understand what she has to do and what you're up against. But whether she is military or not, the most important thing is she has to be someone you trust . . . with your life. She has your back.

> **It's very important to find someone, preferably another military wife, who will stick with you when the going gets tough. Soldiers call this person a "battle buddy."**

My best friend Sara was, and is, my battle buddy. Her husband was in the Army, too. We made a pact: if something happened to either one of our husbands, we'd be there.

And she *was* there when I really needed her.

After Dan called and said he was wounded, the next call I made was to Sara. She had just returned home to Fort Sill from a trip to New York.

"Have you unpacked yet?" I said to her.

"Yeah," she replied.

"Damn!"

"Why?"

"You've gotta pack again."

"Why?"

"You've gotta come down here to Fort Hood."

"Why?"

"Dan got shot."

"What!"

"Dan got shot."

"You're shittin' me!"

"No, Dan got shot."

"Really?"

"Yes, Dan got shot."

"I'm leavin' in the morning!"

ASK QUESTIONS, TAKE CONTROL OF YOUR TREATMENT

When I had my first child, Billy, I was still a teenager. I didn't know what to do, I didn't know who to talk to, I didn't know the exact questions to ask or anything. I learned much later, with my second and third children, that you have to ask questions. Do some research. Know your options.

Three months before I delivered my first child, one of the nurses asked me, "Are you involved in the teen program?" I hadn't even heard about it! Once they got me in to see the teen OB/GYN, things were a lot better. I wasn't ignorant about childbirth, but having a person there who would talk to me in a way I could understand just made me feel more comfortable. I wish I had known about the program earlier.

When I had Christian, a few years later, I knew what to ask. Questions like:

What can I expect the doctors to do at each stage of the pregnancy? What is the schedule?

What will we do at three months, at five months, at six? When it actually comes down to having the baby, where am I going to go? Under normal circumstances, who will deliver the baby?

And then ask, "Okay, if things don't go well, what is the procedure?"

DEALING WITH LANDSTUHL

There are also some important things to ask when your husband is the patient. If there is an overseas deployment, you might hear that injured soldiers first fly to Landstuhl Regional Medical Center in Germany.

Before your spouse deploys, get the current phone numbers for Landstuhl! After my husband was injured, I called an 800 number for the Army in the Washington, D.C. area, trying to find out what was going on. They had no flipping idea! No idea. He should have landed in Germany five hours earlier, and they said, "Oh, well, he's in the barracks. He should be calling you."

"You're telling me that in less than twenty-four hours, my husband has been taken off a machine that's giving him pain medicine and put in the barracks!"

"Yeah, that's what we're showing; he's in the barracks."

They didn't know what they were talking about! Sara and I got on the Internet and found the phone number for the hospital at Landstuhl.

We called, and they said, "Yes, he's here. He's in the ICU right now. He's fine, he's stable, he's sleeping." They promised to have him call me when he woke up. They were great. I wish I had tried that number in the first place.

After my husband was flown from Landstuhl to Fort Hood, Texas, he stayed in the local hospital for another two or three weeks. He had several different surgeries, cleaning things out, putting rods in his arm, all sorts of stuff. Then came all the follow-up appointments and rehab. Countless appointments. Countless!

It would have been a nightmare trying to remember all his appointments, not to mention mine and the kids'. Those little computer printouts they give you at the clinic listing all your appointments saved our butts more than once. I got in the habit, every morning, of looking at the printout the hospital had given me. Some days it would be, "Oh crap, we have an appointment in forty-five minutes! Dan, get up! We gotta go!"

Those printouts were gold.

SECRET INGREDIENT:
TOGETHER TAKES SHEER DETERMINATION

After Dan returned, wounded, from Iraq, we went through hell. I had the kids with me, and they had problems. Dan was injured, and he had changed. There were many losses in his unit, and one loss particularly hurt him.

He is a very private person, and he kept a lot of stuff in, which was destroying him from the inside. Dan actually filed for divorce during that time. We still loved each other, but we had grown apart.

It took sheer determination on my part not to give up. I called Army OneSource. They were just great. All I had to do was say I needed to see a counselor and they connected me right through to a doctor's office. They stayed on the line until the appointment was arranged, and even called back two or three times after that to follow up and make sure everything was going okay. We received both individual and couples counseling. This got us through the roughest time.

> After Dan returned, wounded, from Iraq, we went through hell.

FAMILY READINESS GROUPS

Family Readiness Groups (FRGs) are organizations that bring together soldiers' loved ones so they will know what is going on in the unit.

The FRG leader is usually the commander's spouse. This can be a good thing or a bad thing. Some wives act like they are wearing their husband's rank. If the first thing out of a woman's mouth is "I'm Colonel So-and-So's wife," I immediately turn off.

But there are some really good people out there, like Leslie, who was the FRG leader when my husband deployed to Iraq. She was our battalion commander's wife, but you would never know it. She was so down to earth, a bluejeans and t-shirt type of person. I never knew her to act like she wore rank or talk down to anybody. She was always sympathetic and listened to what everyone was saying. That's the thing that drew me to her.

So, a word to the wise for all you FRG leaders out there: be approachable. When you're approachable, the younger wives will feel more like being part of the group. Just be a normal everyday kind of person, because if you talk down to them or treat them like they are ignorant, they won't come back.

When my husband's unit was deploying to Iraq, certain meetings were mandatory for families. I went because I knew how important it was to be there in person, to get the information firsthand. I had been through deployments before, when my husband went to Macedonia and Kosovo. I knew the deal: husbands often sugarcoat some things. So, if you want the real scoop, you need to hear it from unit leaders and other spouses.

FINAL COMMENTS

Before marrying a soldier, ask yourself if this is a lifestyle you can handle. You are going to be alone a lot more than you are together most of the time. Be prepared. It's a lifestyle choice, and you must be ready to deal with it. Be organized, with all your paperwork and everything that you need.

Personally, I wouldn't have missed it for the world.

BETH KAMPHAUS KNOTTS

"Know your rights as well as your responsibilities."

Beth, a native of Boston, Massachusetts, studied journalism and television production at Xavier University in Cincinnati, Ohio. She spent most of her senior year covering all the 1991 Gulf War happenings as an intern for a local TV station, never dreaming she herself would one day have intimate dealings with the military. Today, she is the wife of a lieutenant colonel who teaches ROTC at Eastern Illinois University and the proud mom of three Army brats.

IN THE BEGINNING

When I was studying journalism at Xavier, I felt like my future was laid out before me. I was destined to cover all the great stories of my generation. Little did I know that every once in a while, God says, "HA!" and throws you a curve ball.

While moving into a new apartment, my roommates bumped into an Army lieutenant friend who was in town on leave. He had just been dumped by his girlfriend, so they offered him a place to crash in return for some heavy lifting during the move.

I came home from work that evening to find a handsome, soft-spoken guy named Stephen in our living room. During the move we had a couple of fun days of talking, good food and laughter, but alas, duty called and he had to fly to Hawaii for his first station in Field Artillery.

I wasn't looking for a husband. I hadn't sweated through four years of university to get my "Mrs." degree. But there I was, with that lump in my throat as he prepared to exit my life.

"I'll write you," he said.

"Sure you will," I said doubtfully. And what do you know? Seventeen years later he still does! I never expected any of that.

We dated, long distance, for three years. That wasn't easy! I think what probably kept us most connected were the letters. I have boxes and boxes of letters. At least weekly, and sometimes daily, I would get a letter from him. It was not anything special, just whatever he was doing at the time. When he was welcomed into his new unit in Hawaii, they gave him a lei. He took one of the orchids off his lei and pressed it into the letter and sent it to me. When Stephen would be on an Army training exercise I would get letters with red clay dirt on them (from the field environment they were in), and he would draw little pictures and write me little songs. I kept all of these.

They tell a story and bring back wonderful memories. Never throw away the things that keep you connected.

When he was not on a field exercise (also called an "FTX"), we talked on the phone. We probably had thousands of dollars of phone bills, but it was too important to worry about the expense. The reality was that we were planning to spend our lives together, so we needed to invest in the relationship up front. So we talked, often, and dealt with the important issues before they became burdens.

MAKING A LIVING

EASIER TO ASK FORGIVENESS THAN TO BEG PERMISSION

Everywhere you go there will be rules, lots of rules! They cover everything from where you can park or shop to who can receive benefits as a family member. Most rules are important and keep people safe and things in order.

But some of them are just plain stupid. We ran into one of those rules when I came to visit Stephen in Hawaii. It is a long, expensive trip, so I planned to visit for almost three weeks. It would have been totally unaffordable for me to stay in a hotel the entire time, so I stayed with Stephen in his quarters on post. He slept on the couch while I slept in the bed. But the rules at that time said you couldn't have overnight guests in the BOQ (Bachelor Officer Quarters) unless they were family. Someone ratted him out that there was a girl in his quarters, so somewhere in Hawaii there is a piece of paperwork in a housing office that says I'm his cousin.

NEVER MAKE HARD AND FAST PLANS

We made all sorts of wonderful plans for a winter wedding at Aberdeen in Maryland. This was the perfect spot for a young ordnance officer to marry his bride. The Army, however, didn't cooperate. The day before

Thanksgiving Stephen called me and said, "I've got good news and I've got bad news. The good news is, the captains list came out and I'm on it!"

Yay! He was going to be promoted!

"The bad news is my unit is going to Haiti just after the New Year. We have to postpone the big church wedding."

The entire wedding was already planned and everything was paid for. Our wedding invitations were supposed to go out the Monday after Thanksgiving. We talked to the vendors and postponed everything until August.

But Stephen's commander took him aside and said, "You need to bring her here and get married now."

This would ensure I would be taken care of legally on the off chance that something should happen to him.

So Stephen flew me to Hawaii, and we made plans to be married by a judge in Honolulu. Stephen thought, "We'll just go do the legal thing, no big deal. We're having the big event in August, so there is no need for anything special." A Marine Corps sergeant's wife named Trish taught me all the ropes of military living. This was one of the first moments she stepped up and said, "That's absolutely not acceptable! This is *your wedding*."

> **Even if plans change or must be adjusted at the last minute, make everything special. The memories exist for a lifetime.**

I didn't bring any formal wear, so she gave me a beautiful dress to wear. Trish also made me a silk bouquet of flowers. It was Christmastime, so she put little Christmas lights in it. She and her husband were our witnesses, and they threw us a dinner that night with presents and everything. Her husband (the Marine Corps sergeant) made our wedding cake. These two wonderful people taught us a very valuable lesson. Even if plans change or must be adjusted at the last minute, make everything special. The memories exist for a lifetime.

DEPLOYMENTS

Seventeen days after our wedding, Stephen picked up his M16 rifle, kissed me goodbye and deployed to Haiti. It was his first deployment, but it was also my baptism by fire.

I decided to stay in Hawaii for the duration. I was lucky to have Trish to show me the ropes. She took me under her wing and introduced me to the concept of Family Readiness Groups and the Officers' Wives Club. It was quite an education. Every Army wife quickly learns about Murphy's Law: anything that can go wrong will go wrong. It certainly did.

> The key for a military spouse during a deployment is to spend your time helping somebody else.

Shortly after my groom reached Haiti and settled into his job for Operation Uphold Democracy, my parents were in a devastating car accident. I flew back to Florida to help out. My dad was in the hospital, and my mom was ill with Parkinson's. That was a very difficult time, but Stephen's commanders made sure he was able to contact me and that I had everything I needed.

Once I returned to Hawaii, the time passed excruciatingly slowly. I missed him so much. After three long years, we were finally married, and now he was gone! I discovered that the key for military spouses during a deployment is to spend your time helping somebody else.

That person for me was Trish. She had had multiple miscarriages and also had a baby die at eight weeks. Two days after I returned to Hawaii she said, "I need to go to Tripler [the hospital]. I took a pregnancy test and it's negative, but my period is late."

"When did you take it?" I asked.

"Last week."

"Well, take another one."

"I have to wait 'til payday or go to Tripler."

She was a sergeant's wife, and they don't have a lot of money. So I bought her a test, and she took it in my bathroom. I was the first one to know my future goddaughters were on their way! From then on, I spent a lot of time taking her to her doctors' appointments because she was considered a high risk pregnancy. Having someone else to focus on instead of focusing on my own loneliness was huge.

OTHER WAYS TO STAY SANE

Have a weekly routine you can count on. Don't look too far ahead over the long, long months of separation. Instead, look forward to the weekly events on your schedule. During later deployments I discovered it is especially important to have a routine with kids. They need to have some semblance of order in their lives, something they can count on.

In Hawaii every Saturday night I would go to mass at Soldier's Chapel. Then on Sunday I would drive up to the north shore and have a shave ice at Matsumoto's, which is the best place on the island to get that treat. I would sit on the sand and slowly eat my shave ice. It was something I looked forward to every week.

MAKING MARRIAGE AND FAMILY WORK

Marriage is work. Marriage isn't a cakewalk. This isn't the movies or some bad TV show on the Lifetime network. Being an Army wife is not for the faint of heart. Marriage on its best days takes a lot of effort. I have heard some wives say, "Oh my kids are the most important thing. My husband comes second." Well if you are not happy in your marriage, then how are your kids going to be happy?

Stephen is remarkable at keeping us connected during a deployment.

Three words in an email, a few cards, a few letters, that's all it would take to sustain me, but he does so much more. After a three-year tour in Germany, our family had added the tradition of leaving out our shoes for St. Nicholas to fill on December 5th. Good people get candy, money and oranges; the naughty get sticks. So when he was deployed Stephen arranged for a neighbor to fill my Kris Kringle shoe. He would also have my best friend wrap my Christmas presents for me, or go and get flowers for my birthday! These things kept me going.

Stephen and I often made "dates" to walk outside at midnight Kuwaiti time (10 p.m. Central European Time) so we could look at the constellation Orion together. The girls will always remember that he called on Christmas Eve so he could read *'Twas the Night Before Christmas* to them, and that he would also take five minutes out of his day to call their school and have them brought to the office to "talk to their dad, who is deployed." We worked really hard to keep the kids connected to their dad. We got through it together.

REUNION

Eventually Stephen came home. I made cookies. I cleaned the house. I bought all his favorite foods for great romantic dinners. I got my hair cut and bought a new outfit. I did everything I thought a wife needed to do to properly welcome her soldier home.

But in the end, none of that mattered. What mattered was that he was home. I could hold his hand and wake up next to him. All the peripheral stuff everybody thinks they should do is not important. What's important is keeping it together while he's gone. If you don't work on keeping your marriage together, if it is not a priority for both of you, then you are going to have issues. The hair, the dress, the cleaning, the special dinner—not important! The fact that you are there, he is there, and you both *want* to be there, that's important.

MAKING A LIFE

DAY TO DAY SECRETS

It is *so* important to be able to ask for help when you need it, and I am really bad at reaching out to people when I need help. Because I am stubborn, I just try to do it myself. There are friends and neighbors just waiting for you to ask. So ask!

Get involved in your unit. Volunteering is huge, and it really helps pass the time when deployments or field exercises keep your husband away. I have been the "layette" representative (taking a baby gift to new mothers in the unit), an emergency babysitter, a labor coach and a volunteer for the bazaar in Heidelberg.

> **Give your best and be proud that you have helped someone. Don't let one or two naysayers convince you that you are not doing a good job.**

I have also run three Family Readiness Groups (FRGs). My first one, when Steve was a company commander, was a nightmare. I let myself be bullied by someone who was never happy about anything. We were trying to include everyone in the group. We had taken care of our soldiers and families through three rotations to the National Training Center in California, but nothing I was doing seemed good enough for her. I almost quit. But I found out everyone else thought I was doing a phenomenal job. It was just this one person who was dissatisfied.

Give your best and be proud that you have helped someone. Don't let one or two naysayers convince you that you are not doing a good job.

FRIENDS ARE THE ULTIMATE SECRET

Be open to making friends. Trish and Janet became like family to me. In fact, for all intents and purposes, I was married to Janet Morris for a year. My husband was gone with the Corps Support Command, and her husband Todd was gone with Corps Artillery, the unit my husband had just left. They have two sons, we have three daughters. Stephen left in September, Todd left in December. When Stephen was gone, Todd was there to pick up the slack for my daughters. Then he left, and in May Stephen came home for his mid-tour leave. We included the Morrises in everything we did. Then Stephen went back to Iraq, and Todd came home in July. You see how it worked? Two families became stronger by supporting each other. Find a good friend, preferably someone in a similar situation. Your friends become your family.

LIVING ON POST

I like living on a military post. When I am not able to, I miss the camaraderie. Stephen's current assignment is Senior Military Science Instructor for a small midwestern university. There are no military posts nearby, so we live in the community. It's like being Amish out among the English living here. I speak a different language. People here have no idea what my life is like. And it is such a small town that it can be very difficult to make friends. They know I'm temporary, so why bother? In a military community, everybody is temporary. You become very close very fast.

In a military community, everybody is temporary. You become very close very fast.

CHILDREN AND MOVING

Our kids seem to have really weathered all the deployments and moves without issues. We've always talked about moving as an adventure. We would remind the kids that it is an opportunity to see somewhere new, make new friends, do new things and experience different people and cultures.

When we moved to Germany, my kids could walk down to the *Bäckerei* (bakery) and buy our *Brötchen* (German hard rolls) and go over to the *Metzgerei* (meat shop) and buy our *Kinderwurst* and *Schinken* (sausage and ham). This was great for our girls. They were very adept at communicating with the locals. All the German merchants knew my kids, who were very polite, and the merchants loved it when they came into their stores. The girls loved it too.

> **Moving is an adventure, and living overseas was an added adventure**

Moving is an adventure, and living overseas was an added adventure. Now that Stephen is retiring, we will have a whole new adventure awaiting us!

Another way we helped our children adjust throughout all the trials of military life was to just let them be themselves. This made a huge difference. We don't seem to have any of the traditional sibling rivalry or competition in our family because we embrace what is different about our kids. No one is forced to play the same sports or do the same activities. This prevents some of the competition I have seen in other families. Just embrace the differences in your family. Differences are what make things beautiful. Life would be pretty boring if rainbows were all one color.

RECOMMENDATIONS FOR NEW MILITARY FAMILIES

Army Family Team Building (AFTB) is fantastic. "AFTB Level One" is like "Army 101." They teach you how to read your husband's pay statement. They will teach you the rank and the structure of the military. It's a very basic class, but essential.

They will also teach you some acronyms. The Army has an acronym for everything! Get to know the basic ones or you will think people are speaking a foreign language. I convinced all my young soldiers' wives to take that class. Every one of them loved it.

I said it before: get involved. Volunteer at the hospital. Volunteer at Fisher House or with Army Emergency Relief. There are all kinds of opportunities. Get involved with your Family Readiness Group. I have a talk with our ROTC cadets every year when they are seniors. I tell them, "Get involved with your FRG. You will know your soldiers better. The spouses of your squad members will be an asset to you. When you need help, your FRG will be there for you."

ARMY FAMILY TEAM BUILDING LEVEL ONE

- Like taking an Army 101 course.
- Basic but essential class

YOU LEARN

- How to read your husband's pay statement
- Rank & structure of the military
- Acronyms

A FINAL PIECE OF ADVICE

Truth be told, the Army's going to tell you whatever they think will accomplish what they need. You have to be educated and informed. You need to know your rights as well as your responsibilities. Sometimes, if they think it will make you go away, they are going to give you misinformation.

Do some research. Know your rights and stand up for yourself.

When my friend Trish was pregnant with the twins, she asked for a "statement of non-availability" from the hospital. This would allow her to see a civilian doctor for her pregnancy because she was so high risk. We had to go talk to the insurance office to see if the request had been processed. When we asked the lady at the desk if any decision

Just because someone outranks you doesn't mean they aren't wrong.

had been made, she said "Congress vetoed your request."

Trish was dumbfounded. I looked at the lady and said, "Do you really think she is that stupid? Don't stand here and tell her Congress vetoed her request. Tell her the truth and give her the information she needs to move on."

Do some research. Know your rights and stand up for yourself. Absolutely stand up for yourself. I tell our cadets that. You have to know the facts. And just because someone outranks you doesn't mean they aren't wrong.

KAREN BOOTH

"Home is the experiences you've had, the friends you've made, and all your memories along the way."

Because Karen Booth's family lived next to the United States Military Academy in West Point, she grew up thinking the military was a place of beautiful buildings and old cannons to climb on. Then she fell in love with Brad Booth, who coincidentally turned out to be a graduate of West Point. He is currently stationed at Fort McNair as the Deputy Chief of Staff at the National Defense University. Karen and Brad have two teenage daughters, Kaitlin and Kelly.

IN THE BEGINNING

I grew up next to the United States Military Academy at West Point, New York—also known as USMA, Army, The Academy or The Point. It's the Army's four-year service academy where all cadets are commissioned as second lieutenants upon graduation. It also exudes military history with impressive historical architecture.

My first impression of the military was sitting on the cannons at Trophy Point. West Point is overflowing with history and the architecture is a sight to behold!

MAKING A LIVING

MILITARY LIFE

When Brad and I got engaged, Brad talked to me about "life in the Army." He wanted me to understand that it's not like civilian life. I really didn't listen clearly to all of that. All that mattered, really, was *I was in love!* I am an adventurous individual and I don't remember being worried about the new lifestyle I was entering into. I was just excited to get married to the most wonderful man in the world!

Reality hit even before the wedding—two weeks before, to be precise—which was when we had to cancel our wedding because Brad's unit was deploying to

> I realized that an Army wife must be flexible enough to change plans in a heartbeat and make the best of "Plan B" because sometimes "Plan B" becomes "Plan C, D, E . . ."

Somalia. After a minor breakdown on my part and the loss of fifteen pounds (also on my part), we ended up being married by a justice of the peace a week earlier than we had planned. From that point on, I realized that an Army wife must be flexible enough to change plans in a heartbeat and make the best of "Plan B" because sometimes "Plan B" becomes "Plan C, D, E . . ."

TIGHT QUARTERS

I have always preferred living on post rather than off post. Living on post helps me feel more of a part of the Army community, and it is much easier to form friendships when everyone around you is in a similar situation.

Here is my personal secret about Army housing; no matter what the building looks like or how small or large it is, make it a home for you and your family. I always look for the potential in the house, and then I turn it into our home. Painting can add that extra personal touch to the cold, white, hospital-like walls.

> No matter what the building looks like or how small or large it is, make it a home for you and your family.

When settling in to a new house, set the kitchen up first! Usually during a PCS (Permanent Change of Station) move, you and the family have been eating out for a few weeks while traveling and waiting in a hotel for your house to be ready. Having your first home-cooked meal in your new house is one step closer to feeling normal again.

An awesome thing about moving so many places is that our furniture has history. I can tell you where every piece of furniture came from. Each piece has a story, a country or a state that is associated with it. Some pieces still have moving stickers on them from four moves ago!

Don't let yourself get isolated because you don't know anyone when you move. Find your niche right away. Mine was Army Family Team Building (AFTB). AFTB helps you understand the functions of the Army and the soldier's role. They also help you create a higher level of self-sufficiency during times of separation. I took all the classes, became an instructor and made wonderful friends that I remain close to today.

> **Don't let yourself get isolated because you don't know anyone when you move. Find your niche right away.**

Organizations and groups will help you feel like a huge part of the military community and not so alone. Remember, knowledge is power, so use all the services offered and read all the literature you may get.

DEPLOYMENTS

Brad was deployed three times during the course of our marriage. Each deployment was unique, and my needs and concerns were different in all three situations.

When Brad first deployed, we had recently married, and I was a "company commander's spouse" with no clue of what was expected of me in my newfound leadership role. After a few tears and the realization I needed to ask for help, I made it through with flying colors.

The next deployment was several years later. Kaitlin and Kelly were eight and six years old, and we were stationed in Rheindahlen, Germany, on a British installation. My concerns were not related to understanding Army life; this time, I was most worried about finding my way to the nearest commissary: a one-hour drive through little towns, winding roads and into another country, the Netherlands. So I bought myself a GPS—every Army wife should own one!

The latest deployment was just a year and half ago. After spending two years in Korea, Brad was given orders to deploy to Afghanistan. We decided that the girls and I would live in the D.C. area while Brad was away. This deployment held many different challenges; the girls were much older, and transferring from one school to another and leaving their friends behind became much more difficult.

My secret during deployments? Keep busy! Set goals for you and your kids, create special activities, visit family often or have them visit you. Get involved with groups and organizations. Before you know it, the year will be over and your soldier will be coming home!

REUNIONS

Reunions are incredible, especially when you get to pick your soldier up at the gate in the airport. It can be very emotional to say the least.

After the celebratory part of the reunion, life is not back to normal with the family. For the past year, Mom has been the "go to" parent, taking care of everything. All of a sudden, the family members get confused about the roles of the mom and dad. It's time to readjust back to the way it was before the deployment.

For the past year, Mom has been the "go to" parent, taking care of everything. All of a sudden, the family members get confused about the roles of the mom and dad.

The post-deployment period can be just as difficult as the deployment itself. My secret? Communicate with one another and know that it is okay to feel stressed about the spouse being back home. Don't bottle it up or feel like there is something wrong with you. Talk it out!

MAKING A LIFE

TRAVEL

The military has given our family so many opportunities to travel the world. We have been to the Eiffel Tower in Paris. (Kaitlin and I were too chicken to go to the very top, but Brad and Kelly own the bragging rights for that one.) We have climbed over 1,700 steps on the Great Wall of China, and we have been inside the tomb of Ramses in Egypt's Valley of the Kings. Kaitlin actually spent her tenth birthday in Egypt! Our family has walked the ancient grounds of Knossos in Greece, and we have stood on the cliff in Saipan where thousands of Japanese met their deaths.

Remember that each time you move it's going to be a new experience. Take it for all it's worth and run with it. You won't regret it!

HOME

Of course, with all the moving, new friends will ask, "Where are you from?" My kids still get confused on that one. Are they from the state where they were born or where we live now? Kaitlin was born in California, but we moved when she was only eight months old; Kelly was born in Washington State, and we moved when she was only three. I told them that they are from all over. Home does not have to be one particular place. Home is the experiences you had, the friends you made, and all your memories along the way.

> **Home does not have to be one particular place. Home is the experiences you had, the friends you made, and all your memories along the way.**

MY OWN CAREER

I graduated from the State University of New York at Albany with a bachelor's degree. I also received a teaching degree from Mount Saint Mary's College and a master's degree in organizational leadership from Chapman University. I am currently teaching elementary school and enjoy every minute of it. With all the moves, teaching has provided me with a much-needed outlet and a special place just for me outside of military life. Being a teacher is a great job for an Army spouse since teachers are needed all over the world. I have taught in New York, California, Georgia, Germany, Korea and now Virginia. Besides being a mom and Army wife, teaching is one of the things I love to do.

LINDA VANVRANKEN

"Being older helped me navigate with a different perspective."

Linda was the divorced mother of grown children when, much to her surprise, she fell in love with a soldier and became an Army bride. Some may see uniqueness in Linda and Russ's marriage because they are twenty-five years apart in age; but they share a love of life and a deep appreciation of the military life.

Linda currently considers herself not only an Army wife but also a singer, chef, comedian and writer. Besides being married to Sergeant First Class Russ VanVranken, she is mother to Lori, Jimmy and Jay, and grandmother to James, Johnny, Joey, Jace, J. Dylan and Taylor.

IN THE BEGINNING

I was born in Pennsylvania. My maternal grandparents emigrated from Austria and only spoke Ukrainian. I was very blessed to have a unique childhood surrounded by the Ukrainian culture, food and religion of my parents. My father was in the Army, and my ex-husband, who has now passed on, was in Vietnam as an Infantry First Lieutenant.

I met Russ seventeen years ago while having dinner with friends. As our conversation progressed, he asked me out for a drink. Stunned, I mentioned I was old enough to be his mother—and seriously, I was.

He quickly responded with, "I didn't ask you how old you are but if you would like to have a drink."

To this day I am not sure how I responded after that.

We did have a drink, and we enjoyed each other's company. At first, I never thought it would turn into anything more than that. Some of my friends said that they went through a period of dating younger men after their divorce and told me to just enjoy it and have fun; but the fun turned into more—we fell in love.

> **Keep all the contact numbers, paperwork and significant documents like passports in order and have easy access to it all.**

Needless to say, both of us were scared, unsure and questioning. We had to face many "are you kidding me?" looks. The most important—and the most frightening—thing was explaining our engagement to my children and his family. What, I have not mentioned the age difference of twenty-five years? Yes, you read that correctly! Age for us is a number; Russ is an old soul and I am a young spirit and we meet in the middle. I know that we will face the future together and take what comes because of our love.

MAKING A LIVING

DEPLOYMENTS

Deployment did not affect our lives until 9/11 when Russ was activated. His duty was still in Arizona, so that transition was relatively easy—until his first deployment to Afghanistan in 2006. Then I got a true taste of military life.

Russ headed to Fort Hood, Texas, for training before the deployment. Originally we were told we could go to Fort Hood with our soldiers. Then after some of us rented apartments, we were told we could not go. Janet Napalatano, governor of Arizona at the time, intervened on the families' behalf. We could go but would have to live off post. So I chose to get an apartment off post so that we could be near each other during the eight months of training before he left for the year-long deployment in Afghanistan.

In hindsight, I wish I'd been more prepared. Do your homework; keep all the contact numbers, paperwork and significant documents like passports in order and have easy access to it all. It's important to have contact people as well; someone to call in case you need help of any kind.

REENLISTNG

While deployed in Afghanistan, Russ talked more and more about making the Army his career. Russ wanted to reenlist; so as a husband and wife should do, we discussed it. We looked at all the positives and negatives— and the Army won. It was hard to believe at my age I was now an official army wife, the wife of a noncommissioned officer. This means that my husband did not go to any of the academies, or Officer Candidate School. When Russ was deployed with the National Guard, I really had not yet experienced Army life. I was living in our home in Phoenix, and it had been just the inconvenience of weekend training and two weeks a summer until the first deployment to Afghanistan. I went from civilian to Army wife quickly, and we moved on post. Our first post was Fort Hood, and our new duty location will be Schofield Barracks, Hawaii. Aloha!

JOINING THE FAMILY

I was not sure how I would be received into the close-knit Army family. Even though I was very secure in my marriage, I was not the typical young Army wife. To be significantly older and not have any knowledge of the Army lingo and rules was more than a little intimidating. I have never had any issue relating to people. I am pretty outgoing and really live life in today. I keep up on music, all kinds, the latest styles, what's trending, as they say. This isn't the real worth of a person, but it keeps me current, and it's fun!

I felt very comfortable with the soldiers, wives, and everything that goes with it while I was with Russ in the National Guard. The eight months of training where we were together at Fort Hood went very quickly, but then when it came time for him to leave and fly to Afghanistan, it was hard and the year following did not go by so quickly.

Once training was over and Russ was in Afghanistan, I went back to Russ and my home in Phoenix, Arizona. This way, I was surrounded by my kids and grandchildren. I had all the comforts of being in our shared home; I also had my family very near.

Each day left a hole in my heart with Russ being gone. He didn't have family and friends there for him; he couldn't just go out of town for the weekend, or go to dinner or just have a glass of wine. He had to be on call 24/7; lives were in his hands. He was in a war, and I was in the Arizona sun.

MAKING A LIFE

BEING CREATIVE WITH SMALL QUARTERS

After Russ reenlisted, we moved on post. This meant that we moved from a home with nearly 3,700 square feet to a duplex of 972 square feet. Well, *that* has been fun!

My furniture is rather large, and I insisted certain pieces were going in the Army with us. I tell my friends their first visit to our home requires them signing a release which states they will not sue us for medical damages if they bump into any of our furniture. We were assigned quarters, packed up and arrived to move in, sight unseen—except for a photo of the front of the house that caused me to say, "Well, I definitely don't want *that* one!" (I, of course, wanted one of the newer townhouses, with more space.) But "that one" it was.

This house does have a large yard and great neighbors, plus it's quiet and very old. I imagine the size to be what you would find in a quaint New York apartment.

My passion is cooking, and the majority of our moving boxes contained kitchen necessities—lots of them. Being creative helps! Our kitchen is very small with barely any cabinet space. A soldier came over once, saw a large tool chest in our kitchen, and commented that he was surprised to find out that Russ is into tools!

Utilize your space well; it really does make a difference.

Nope, we explained, he isn't—the tool chest is used for spices, silverware, kitchen equipment and, of course, as a conversation starter!

Utilize your space well; it really does make a difference. However small, our home is perfect because it has the most important ingredients: lots of love and us.

THE HOMEFRONT DURING DEPLOYMENT

I believe that the spouse's job during deployment is to run the home, take care of the finances and handle family business. It's important to me to handle what needs to be handled. Russ doesn't need to worry about me or what is happening at home—he needs to focus and concentrate on his job there. There is nothing he can do anyway, so why worry him?

I had a medical issue and did not tell my husband. The only thing he could have done was worry. Of course, there are exceptions, but my rule of thumb is to ask: Can I handle it? If not, can it wait? Can I deal with it now, or can it wait to be handled when he gets home?

It's important to let our soldiers know that while they are gone we care and think of them every single day!

For younger wives with children, I tell them to prepare themselves the very best they can to be single parents when their spouses are deployed. Try to work on a good support system, with both your personal families and your Army families. I know it is hard to raise children without that constant communication with your spouse and that support.

I sometimes think that I was able to handle the deployment more easily because we do not have small children. That is when my heart goes out to my fellow Army husbands and wives. It is a challenge we did not have to face. But to those who do, make sure you have friends who also have children so you can take turns watching each other's kids to get a break.

I also think being older may help me navigate through life with a different perspective. I have raised children, had a career and have learned that today is the most important day you have; live life each day to the fullest.

I also sent a continual flow of goodies over to my husband along with letters and photos so he would not get lonely. It's important to let our soldiers know that while they are gone we care and think of them every single day!

MISTAKES

First, we are all human and we will make mistakes along the way. What we do with those mistakes is what will make a difference; learn from them!

Once, I asked my husband if I had made any real mistakes as an Army wife; of course, being a good husband, he said no. But I have a tendency to call people "honey," so there have been majors and colonels whom I have "honeyed." Fortunately, they have turned out to be some of the people I count as very special friends. (That said, it is not appropriate to "honey" majors and colonels!)

I have never had any issue with any of the Army family members or Army wives in our unit or any other; my experience has been wonderful! Maybe the only mistake I made is that we didn't join the Army sooner.

POIGNANT MOMENTS

Stepping on post fills me with so many emotions: pride, admiration, amazement and reverence. Every day, I still feel so blessed to live here. It's impossible to drive around post and not feel respect and devotion for our soldiers.

I'll never forget the first time I was driving, and, suddenly, cars began to stop, and people emerged from their cars and faced the flag. Some were saluting, some holding their hand over their hearts.

I discovered that on some Army posts, at certain times of the day, the bugle will sound over the loudspeakers and play the song appropriate for that time of day; early morning is "Revelry" and at the end of the day, "Taps." "Taps" is sounded at dusk and at funerals by the U.S. military. Remember when you hear that music on post that it is important to acknowledge it and pay the proper respect. It instills in us why we are Army wives. I still get chills when I hear it. It's an experience every American should have.

CHOOSING TO BE HAPPY

I think the secret of getting through a deployment, a move, and almost everything you do in life is attitude. You can look at each move as a new chapter and with that chapter comes new friends and new surroundings. You can choose to be happy or you can choose to be miserable. That doesn't mean you won't have difficult times, painful times, lonely times. That's life. We all face these things.

> I try to wake up every day thankful for being alive and choose to be happy.

I try to wake up every day thankful for being alive and choose to be happy. When you practice it enough, it starts to come easy. Now if that only worked for being skinny, I would think my happy thoughts right into my skinny jeans!

The bottom line is that I love being an Army wife, love the Army life and feel very blessed and privileged to be part of the Army family.

DONNA HAMILL

"The reserve soldier's greatest challenge is time."

Donna is an elementary school teacher in Augusta, Georgia. She met her husband, Sergeant First Class Brent Hamill, after he had already served for seventeen years as an Army Reserve soldier.

Donna's father was a civilian lawyer who spent many years with an additional job as a Judge Advocate General (JAG) officer for the New York Army National Guard. But this had little impact on day-to-day family life, and Donna had little awareness of her father's military service. Life as a child in New York followed by undergraduate and graduate school at Georgia Southern University did little to prepare her for the new language and lifestyle she would experience when she met Brent. They were married in 2010 and have a young son, James Hugh Hamill.

MAKING A LIVING

WELCOME TO THE ARMY

When Brent and I were dating, his military schedule was very predictable. We both lived in Augusta, Georgia, and his Army Reserve unit, 359th Signal BDE, was right here in town. He didn't have to travel far for his military duty one weekend a month or for his two weeks of annual training each year. It was all pretty straightforward, and I knew we could handle it.

So we decided to get married and began planning a wedding about eight months away. Then one day he came home and said, "Sweetie, you're gonna hate me, but . . ."

His unit's planned deployment had been moved up, and they were now scheduled to leave about the time we were planning to get married. Originally, the wedding was going to be up in New Jersey so both our families could easily get there. Instead, we eloped. He and I flew to Aruba (with our parents' blessings), along with our two best friends, and got married. We came home and had a big family party.

I was not prepared for any of this. We got married, and three months later he was leaving on a deployment. Wow, I didn't really realize what was happening until suddenly he was gone.

YELLOW RIBBON PROGRAMS

Fortunately, the Army has special programs to help Reserve families get the resources they need when their soldiers are away on deployments. The most helpful things for me were the Yellow Ribbon programs, a series of learning events at a local hotel where they talked about everything from insurance to pay issues, powers of attorney, anger management, how to contact the unit in case of an emergency, you name it! This was a "one-stop shopping" event that enabled the families of the deploying soldiers to connect with other families. It was great camaraderie, and all the vendors were really helpful.

GETTING THROUGH DEPLOYMENTS

My husband was not new to overseas assignments and deployments. He had gone overseas to Germany, Egypt, and Iraq before we were together. This was new for me, though, and the biggest thing that helped me get through it was the Family Readiness Group, or FRG.

At our first Yellow Ribbon program, I met the FRG leader, Lisa. She really rocked! She understood the system and was really, *really* helpful. The only problem was she didn't know if she could handle being the FRG leader and was hoping I might take it on. I told her this was not the time for me to step up as leader. I had only been married to the military for three months! But I said, "I'm a very good 'vice,' a good assistant; I will help you."

> I really needed to talk to people who had somebody deployed. They understood, genuinely, what was going on.

We agreed on being co-leaders, and that was probably the best thing I could have done. When I was down in the dumps because I was missing Brent, I found very little comfort from friends and family—whom I love dearly—but who didn't currently have someone deployed.

I really needed to talk to people who had somebody deployed. They understood, genuinely, what was going on. Being part of the FRG support system kept me in contact with others who were going through the same thing. It also helped me keep a positive attitude at a time when the Army had just taken away my husband for a year.

> **When you have to be positive for other people, you tend to think about yourself a little bit less.**

I discovered that when you have to be positive for other people, you tend to think about yourself a little bit less. You can't be "cranky pants" while you're handing the crises faced by other families.

I also recommend that Army Reserve families use the services offered by the YMCA. Active duty soldiers and families usually have gyms and other morale support facilities available for free right on their installations. Reservists may not live close enough to an Army post to make use of those resources. The Department of Defense contracted for free YMCA memberships for deployed Guard and Reserve families. You can go "sweat out" your frustrations at the gym, relax with yoga or go swimming. They offer programs for children, too. Lots of great stuff.

PUT ON YOUR OWN LIFE JACKET FIRST

The most important thing about getting through a deployment is to find a way to do something for yourself. Sometimes, it takes a sneaky best friend to pull this off, because often we don't do well taking care of ourselves. I know of one senior officer who was going to deploy and enlisted his sister to help arrange support for his wife. They passed around a list in which other spouses each signed up to stop by the house once or do something else nice for her. He knew she would never ask for help or anything like that, because most proud Army wives wouldn't, so he and his sister set it up for her.

I kind of wish I set something like that up for myself. After the first few weeks my husband was gone, especially weeks two, three and four, it would have been good to have someone checking in on me.

Another great resource for support during the deployment is the chaplain. Our chaplain was really key. Whenever the unit published an online newsletter, he had an article in there. He always wrote about real stuff that hit home for everybody. He wrote about how the soldiers were feeling and how we at home might be feeling and put it all in perspective. This helped us see things from both sides.

The chaplain also talked about what teenage kids were going through, and as a teacher I really appreciated his observations. I work in a transient elementary school with a large military population, and his insights helped me deal with parents who also had a deployed spouse; it's a very tough dynamic for the parent at home to react "calmly" to an issue at school. It helped me to understand where they were coming from (from 0 to 60 in the blink of an eye) when I remembered what it felt like to be stressed out all of the time!! Those articles from the chaplain definitely helped Brent and me because we would write letters back and forth discussing them.

> Doing something for the unit will help "embrace the suck" . . . That gets you through.

The unit also posted tons of pictures online, which was really cool for someone like me who found it hard to picture what it must be like in Afghanistan. We also had a program through which we sent every member of the unit a Christmas present, all 145 of them! We got to see pictures of the soldiers opening them up. It was really cute. Those newsletters with pictures really helped us stay connected with our deployed soldiers.

The whole situation of being separated from your husband is hard to swallow, but you just have to get through it. So stay connected with your unit through the FRG. Doing something for the unit will help "embrace the suck" as the Army says. That gets you through.

KEEPING IN CONTACT

To keep in contact during the deployment, my husband and I used Skype—when it was working. Sometimes it was really pixilated and hard to see, because the quality totally depends on the Internet connection. My husband traveled a lot with his general, who was helping build roads and schools, so he never knew how the Internet connection was going to be where he was.

We also sent letters to each other. It's old school, but cute. Of course, I also sent care packages: all his favorite goodies—even things you weren't supposed to send. They always asked if there was anything liquid or fragile or hazardous, and I just wrote "shoes and books" on every single package. I figured if they open it and search, they will know what's in it. I wasn't sending anything bad, it's just that Brent likes those Powerade drinks and cookies, and you're not technically supposed to send liquids and food.

REUNION ISSUES

Some couples have problems adjusting to life together after a long, hard deployment. After Brent came home we didn't have any major problems readjusting. Mostly, we had to renegotiate roles, because I had been doing things all on my own while he was gone. But we fell back into line pretty quickly.

Every single couple or family will have some transitional issues after a deployment. It's just a matter of time before it rears its ugly little head in your relationship. So just go and work it out with counseling, before, after or even during the deployment.

I did have to be careful about being too controlling. Brent had had somebody tell him what to do every single waking minute for an entire year. What he really needed now was some independence.

I didn't realize I was doing it, but I would say, "You have to do this and this and this," when what he really wanted was to lay low and do things in his own time.

Before he deployed, he was usually the one who was put out with me because I wouldn't wear a watch and was always ten minutes late for everything. Now I would try to nail down a time for us to do something and he was sort of laissez-faire. I wouldn't say this caused major friction, but sometimes it was an issue.

It took about three to six months before he was back to his old self again. It was probably his civilian job that forced him back on a schedule. After a month of vacation he returned to his former position at AT&T, but they had just lost a manager so he got slammed really hard with work.

CALL MILITARY ONESOURCE

One of the best resources I can recommend to Army families is Military OneSource. Almost anything you need, they can help you find it. Your husband is deployed and suddenly the car breaks in some funky way, and they connect you with someone who can help. Whether you need financial help, tutoring for your kids or even family counseling services, they have it.

During a deployment, it is not a matter of *if* issues are going to pop up, it's *when*. There's always going to be stuff. So check out the Military OneSource. You can use their website, which is really good, but calling is even better. I had heard them give their spiel a hundred times at different events, but it wasn't until I called them and asked for help, that I really

> **MILITARY ONESOURCE CAN HELP YOU FIND ALMOST ANYTHING YOU NEED SUCH AS**
>
> - Financial help
> - Tutoring for your kids
> - Family counseling services
> - Help when your car breaks down
> - And much more

saw how great they were. They said, "Hang on, I'm just going to shoot you over here," and they connected me directly with a person who could help. That sold me. Calling them was really successful.

About the counseling—you get it free, up to twelve sessions! And if you have kids, there are additional free counseling sessions for them.

Brent and I made arrangements to do couples counseling with a pair of psychiatrists we knew. These free sessions helped improve our communication and made Brent's transition home smoother.

I really think this should be part of some checklist for deployment. Every single couple or family will have some transitional issues after a deployment. It's just a matter of time before it rears its ugly little head in your relationship. So just go and work it out with counseling, before, after or even during the deployment. Arrange for it through Military OneSource and it will be paid for.

ARMY LINGO

There is definitely an Army lingo that is different from anything else you may have heard. Army has special terms, codes, and oh my goodness . . .

"Sixteen-hundred *what*??" I know the way they tell time has its own purpose, but I still have to think about it. When someone says "1600," it takes me a few seconds to work the math and figure out they mean 4 p.m.

Even if you get the hang of their lingo very quickly, don't forget the other family members who may struggle with it. If you are putting out fliers or advertisements for events, like an FRG meeting, put times in the twelve-hour-time version (using a.m. and p.m.) We always try to do that with our family member letters. When the information comes out from the unit, the FRG leader and I always change the time format so the families don't have to strain their heads to figure it out.

MAKING A LIFE

SPECIAL CHALLENGES FOR RESERVE SOLDIERS

Time. This is your reserve soldier's greatest challenge. Just time.

There are special ceremonies, or they're preparing for their two-week annual training, and suddenly they have three-day drills instead of two. That takes him out of his civilian job on a Friday, which puts him a little behind there, and he's feeling pressure from his civilian boss.

Brent and I are fortunate that his unit is right here in Augusta and he does not travel. Even so, he leaves the house at six o'clock in the morning and comes home after eight in the evening.

Then, at the end of a weekend in which your husband has been working straight through, spending almost no time with you, he goes back to work on Monday and tries to catch up there.

Yes, time, . . . there is never enough time.

STAND BY YOUR MAN

Your husband really needs your support if he is going to make a go of it in the Army. Army life is not like the show *Army Wives*, but I do think one of the show's main characters, "Claudia Joy," may represent what every Army wife could aim for. It's that "stand by your man" attitude, always supporting him, able to suck it up through the moves, the deployments, all the changes they throw at you. You have to be very resilient.

The Army really does come first. I accept this now and have absolutely no regrets about our relationship.

Brent's activation to deploy was not in my plans, but he has to take orders, and I had to adjust. The Army really does come first. I accept this now and have absolutely no regrets about our relationship. I do wish I had known all this two or three years before the deployment, though.

GENERAL ADVICE

Get involved. Get involved quickly in your unit family activities. And make a good friend, someone who also has a husband in the unit. She will become like a "soul mate" during the deployment. You need someone who understands. I found a lot of comfort in talking with a friend whose husband was deployed. I knew our husbands were working together, so it made us feel connected.

> **I found a lot of comfort in talking with a friend whose husband was deployed. I knew our husbands were working together, so it made us feel connected.**

One Army wife told me she and her best friend from the unit would call on the phone and "share a glass of wine," another one went kayaking with her friend. So, whatever works for you, make a friend.

ADVICE FROM A SCHOOL TEACHER

I want to finish with some observations as a school teacher. I teach in an elementary school that is right next to Fort Gordon, Georgia. We have a lot of students from the post, and so the student population is very transient.

Parents, when you are moving, keep a copy of your child's vaccination records with you. Also, have the addresses and phone numbers of your child's previous schools. And finally, keep an *original* copy of the birth certificate with you. I know that during a move it is really crappy to keep track of all this stuff, but it will make it so much easier to settle into a new school.

If you have a child with special education needs, have a copy of your Individual Education Plan, or IEP. If you are participating in a special education program, you know what I am talking about. The plan should be updated yearly, and it really helps if you show up with it in hand.

I was the special ed chair at my school. When parents came in with an IEP, they were sent over to register with me instead of with the masses of other parents registering. They could be given special care, so it would go much faster and we could handpick the classes for their children.

If you don't have the paperwork, it could take weeks before we get the student's records from a previous school. And if you come from somewhere like Hawaii, it could take even longer, because they don't even start school until two months after we on the mainland do. I'd feel pretty bad if I were a kid sitting in the classroom waiting for two months to get help because the records hadn't shown up!

AND, FINALLY . . .

My husband and I have been married less than three years, and he was deployed one of those years. I don't know what the future has in store, but since I just completed teaching for ten years, I am taking a sabbatical. I'm going to stay home with my husband and my son next year.

JENNIFER LEONARD

"Every assignment offers an opportunity for new experiences, new friends, and new memories."

Jennifer Leonard is a proud Army brat who, much to her surprise, ended up an Army wife. Her life has centered around the military community. The matriarch of a blended family and a military spouse to an officer with duties and responsibilities, she cares deeply about helping other military families in need and takes great pride in her new-found career as a nurse.

IN THE BEGINNING

I am the second and youngest child of Retired Sergeant Major Dave Stroman and Mary Martinson Stroman. We joined my dad in Hawaii when I was three months old; I learned to walk at Schofield Barracks. You know you are an Army brat if you are initially confused when asked where you are from but quickly respond, "Everywhere!"

I graduated from my fifteenth school in Northglenn, Colorado, which was, by the way, my sixth high school. By that time, I was too exhausted to bother with making friends. I spent my time attending the couple of classes I needed to graduate, raising the baby girl I gave birth to between my junior and senior years, and working to support my daughter.

I met Aaron Leonard at a Holiday Inn in Garden City, Kansas, in July of 2002. Aaron was Active Guard and Reserve at the time, and I was working for a medical malpractice insurance company as a medical liabilities analyst. He asked to sit at my table for breakfast. He was very impressed that I recognized his rank of captain. We chatted over the next couple of days. Aaron called me almost a month later, and we met up on our next mutual trip to Garden City. We married on August 5, 2004, in Las Vegas.

The first post I entered as a spouse was Fort Riley, Kansas. It was like coming home. I had not realized how much I missed the familiarity of military life during the five years I spent without a military ID until I stepped back on post to sign for quarters with my husband. As an Army brat, I was comfortable with military life and moves, so I was excited to get back into the military world.

FIRST YEAR FROM HELL

Being a blended family definitely added a level of complexity to military life!

When Aaron and I married, I had two daughters: Kaitlyn, age eleven, and Grace, who was five. Aaron had three daughters: Adara, age twelve, Paige, who was nine, and Ellie, who was seven. It was definitely difficult for the girls to adjust to the additional siblings in their lives! The younger three had a much easier time of it than the older two did. The first year was absolutely the most challenging!

To top it off, Aaron suffered an injury three weeks into our marriage that required bed rest until spinal-fusion surgery was complete—along with a lengthy six weeks of recovery. So I was suddenly a wife, mother of five, nurse to my injured husband, and employee at our local Lutheran church.

To complicate things further, I chose to homeschool my children. As a former Army brat, it was very important to me to give them some level of stability in our fairly unstable lives. On the other hand, Aaron's girls attended out-of-district school, which means they had to be transported to and from school.

I think I asked for a divorce at least every couple of weeks for that first year!

Other issues involved Aaron and his ex-wife having completely different parenting styles than I did. Blending parenting values

The kids have to at least believe that their parent and stepparent are on the same page, even if you are not convinced yourselves.

is certainly one of the hardest aspects of blending families. Each parent believes their style is superior, which instantly causes friction when the kids misbehave. Unfortunately for every blended family, the kids cannot possibly be perfect all of the time and therefore couples have many opportunities in the beginning to butt heads.

I recommend stepping away from the situation when the children get into trouble, take many deep breaths, and try to discuss how to handle the situation with a minimum of negative impact on the child. The kids have to at least believe that their parent and stepparent are on the same page, even if you are not convinced yourselves.

Believe me, all of the girls were more than willing to divide us whenever they saw a weakness in order to get what they wanted. Even cute little five-year-old Grace was more than capable of needling our weak spots for her own benefit.

I highly recommend that any couple thinking of blending their families take a proactive step and find a counselor who specializes in blended families to work out issues before they arise.

We found a blended-family counselor to work with Adara, who had the hardest time. I highly recommend that any couple thinking of blending their families take a proactive step and find a counselor who specializes in blended families to work out issues before they arise. These counselors are out there; it is just a matter of finding the right fit for your family. Do not feel bad if you switch around until you find the right therapist for your family needs, and know that the military has programs that pay for counseling.

We have used the Military OneSource counseling services, which matches a family with a local counselor and will pay for twelve sessions per issue at no cost to the family. We have used this service for couples counseling post-deployment and highly recommend it to military families. TRICARE also offers counseling services to military families.

Although we had many hurdles our first year of marriage, we were able to overcome them and build a strong marriage. Four years into our marriage, Aaron adopted my two girls who have accepted him as their dad. Aaron's middle daughter, Paige, came to live with us full time when she was twelve.

It has been difficult emotionally for Aaron to move around the world without two of his girls, but he is able to visit Adara at college, and Ellie comes to visit us when Aaron is not deployed. We have grown closer as a couple working through the many issues involved in blending our families into one unit. Eight years into our marriage, we are now able to laugh about that first horrific year of marriage. We are a grateful and happy family of seven!

MAKING A LIVING

DEPLOYMENTS

Not only has my husband been deployed, but by the time he came back from his third deployment, he had spent almost half of our seven years of marriage in Iraq. Deployments are definitely the most challenging part of military life. There are dozens of emotions involved and they are all normal. More flexibility is required before, during, and after a deployment than in any other aspect of military life.

> **Deployments are definitely the most challenging part of military life. There are dozens of emotions involved and they are all normal.**

To top it off, every single deployment will be different emotionally, logistically, and parentally. Aaron's first deployment was the scariest for me, the second was the most stressful, and the third deployment was the loneliest.

A strong support system is a must for deployments. Although family is important, the military family you build can be just as valuable. A military family is not biological but adopted. It consists of those military individuals we come to view as family over time. They may be anybody who intimately knows military life and understands

Every single deployment will be different emotionally, logistically, and parentally.

the unique issues involved in day-to-day life that civilians can never truly understand.

A military family member will answer the phone at two o'clock in the morning and tell you that you are completely normal when you woke up in tears because you had a nightmare about your husband who is currently fighting in a combat zone. They might even head over with a bottle of wine in hand. They are the people who bring dinner the night that your spouse deploys and take you to the doctor when you break your toe trying to change the light bulb. They are the people you learn to trust as family.

AFTER-DEPLOYMENT REUNIONS

Here are some basics of what to expect:

- Do accept that you will want to send your (very beloved) soldier back at around the seventy-two hour mark. It's hard to change the role you took on while he was gone. It takes time!

- Do understand that your spouse has experienced things that you will never know or understand. Try not to ask too many questions. Let him know you are willing to listen and then let him come to you when he's ready.

- Do understand that your spouse has spent a lot of time with other soldiers who have become like family for that time. Respect and celebrate those bonds.

- Do know that after an adjustment period, life will settle down to a new normal.

- Don't make plans.

- Don't have ANY expectations.

- Don't set strict schedules.

- Don't think life is suddenly going to be perfect and that all of the problems you had before the deployment will have magically disappeared.

RESOURCES

If you are living on post, some of your best resources are right next door. Your neighbors who have more experience as military spouses are an excellent resource and generally willing to guide you in the right direction! Military OneSource (www.militaryonesource.com) offers tons of articles about different aspects of military life. Through the website you can get many services, including health and wellness coaching and free tax software. On post, Army Community Services (ACS) is a another resource offering financial and deployment-readiness programs. The on-post education office can assist with options for continuing your education. They can explain which colleges offer classes on post and point spouses to the best educational opportunities.

Each installation has a website. Find it! Use it! It will have a wealth of information for the newcomer, from housing options to education and medical information. One of the first things I do when we find out where we are moving is surf the installation's website and make note of all of the information I need to know, as well as any unique benefits offered on post, such as fitness classes, officer's clubs, and church groups for the kids.

MAKING A LIFE

SECRETS TO A SUCCESSFUL MOVE

From a girl who moved seventeen times before graduating from high school and another fourteen times since, I can tell you that successful moves involve high levels of organization! Movers don't care what they are throwing into boxes or if your underwear is packed with your kitchen knives. Put everything you want together into well-labeled plastic boxes, so when they are unpacked on the other side, you can simply slide them into the closet or cabinet and know where they are right away.

> **Movers don't care what they are throwing into boxes or if your underwear is packed with your kitchen knives.**

Also, force your family to eat the foods they've been avoiding by cutting back on the grocery shopping a month before your move. This is a valuable little trick to avoid having to throw out or give away massive amounts of canned peas and frozen chicken breasts the day before the move.

HOW TO SETTLE IN QUICKLY

Let transportation, the moving company, the packers, *and* the driver know you would like your house unpacked by the moving company. That means they have to haul away all of the boxes they unpack. It is so much easier to simply put your things away than to unpack your belongings, put them away, and then have to haul boxes to the drop sight on post.

Always remember that you are in control of your experiences. You can choose to love an assignment as easily as you can choose to hate it. Every single new assignment offers an opportunity for brand new experiences, new friends, and new memories. I meet spouses all the time who hate their current installation and can't wait to leave it. Although I enjoy exploring new places, I try to enjoy where I am at right now, because there are always unique attributes that I can discover about every location.

Whatever your unique interest is, make an effort to locate it as soon as possible at your new assignment. My not-so-unique interest is food. I love the entire experience of eating—the scents, the tastes and the memories food invokes. As soon as I move into my new home, I eat out . . . a lot! I find the best locally owned restaurants, and I eat there often enough that they learn my name and my favorite order. That is my sense of home, no matter where I live.

Find your sense of home and run with it!

LIVING ON POST

I have lived on post and off post, and I personally prefer to live on post. The thing I missed most during those five years without a military ID card was the wonderful sense of community within any installation. In many ways, it is like walking back in time, when communities had a tradition of neighborly behavior. On post, when a new family moves onto the street, there is an expectation that neighbors will introduce themselves and many times bring food.

Living on post is also helpful during times of deployment. I have lived both lifestyles during my husband's deployments, and I believe living on post trumps off post every time! Other military spouses know exactly what is coming, the emotions, and the difficulties of balancing real life and deployment life. They have the ability not only to sympathize, but also to empathize. Spouses living off post during deployments tend to be out of sight and out of mind. That can make a deployment a very lonely time.

LEARNING THE ROPES

I can really only speak to the experience of the officer's spouse entering the military. I think it is important to learn the expectations of being an officer's wife. Purchase a copy of *The Army Wife's Handbook*. Read through it and tab the important information—and feel free to laugh at the ridiculousness of the 1950s mentality.

> I think the biggest mistake I made during my husband's career was thinking that I would fit into the officer's wife mold. I don't, and that's okay.

In my opinion this handbook truly needs to be updated, but it does have quite of lot of valuable information that the normal civilian family doesn't think about. For example, as a wife you should always sit at your soldier's right at a military event. Why, you ask? Because the senior officer should always be at the right of the junior officer, and you always outrank your soldier.

I think the biggest mistake I made during my husband's career was thinking that I would fit into the officer's wife mold. I don't, and that's okay. There are pros and cons to fitting in and there are plenty of us who don't, so it doesn't have to be lonely. You simply have to be willing to keep your eyes open for the other spouses you can relate to.

MY OWN CAREER

I am a licensed practical nurse. I work on the medical/surgical floor of a local hospital and enjoy every minute of it. I love having a career that gives me an identity separate from being an Army wife and mother. Being a nurse is a dream come true, but it has taken many years to achieve due to our multiple moves.

If I had my druthers, I would have gone the whole nine yards and earned a registered nurse degree. But because I am an Army wife who moves around consistently, I chose to take the first step into nursing by entering a one-year licensed practical nurse program. I was able to graduate and have been working for a few months, and now it is time for our next move.

If I am able to get into a program quickly, I will complete my registered nurse degree before we have to move again. It is

> **I love having a career that gives me an identity separate from being an Army wife and mother.**

a challenge that I am more than willing to accept: get in and get through before it is time to move.

I am not a wife who has the ability to stay at home with the kids and maintain any level of sanity. Nursing happens to be a flexible career field and one that I have always dreamed of; fortunately, I have a wonderfully supportive husband who encourages me every step of the way.

MY BIGGEST SECRET!

I will spill the biggest secret to keeping up with Army life. Here goes: write EVERYTHING in pencil because it is likely to change! Be flexible enough to deal with whatever comes your way. This philosophy should be applied to moves, deployments, R&R, your spouse's unit, and on and on. Know that whatever you want to do outside of the military should also be flexible. You should be able to pack up your career, if you choose to have one, and move it anywhere in the world the military may take you.

NANCY NEGRON

"When you marry an Army soldier, you are marrying the Army."

Nancy Negron was born into a large family in Puerto Rico, and just after she joined the military at age seventeen, she began to pursue a bachelor's degree in criminal justice. Nancy, whose husband was also in the Army, worked hard at her job, but worked even harder to juggle her dual military career marriage, because time was so hard to come by.

Through good times and tragedy, Nancy learned that keeping friends and loved ones close is one of the only ways to continue moving forward.

IN THE BEGINNING

I was born in Puerto Rico, a small island in the Caribbean. My extended family is huge; my grandmother had nine children and eight of them have at least one child. We're all very close. Out of all the family, I'm the first and only military member.

I joined the military as a 77F (Petroleum Supply Specialist) in June 1998 when I was seventeen years old. When I came back from basic camp in November 1998, I started college and immediately joined ROTC because I wanted to be an officer and finish my studies at the same time.

It was in ROTC that I met First Lieutenant Carlos J. Diaz Santiago, the man who would become my husband. We got married after his commissioning as a second lieutenant on August 9, 2003.

I finished a bachelor's degree in criminal justice with a minor in criminal investigation from the Inter-American University of Puerto Rico and was commissioned the following year.

MAKING A LIVING

MARRYING THE ARMY

There is a saying that goes, "When you marry an Army soldier, you are marrying the Army." For better or worse, this is true.

When your spouse first goes on active duty, do your best to find out about what he has committed to. When his job becomes very time consuming, remember your spouse is part of a force that is defending and protecting our nation.

You are your soldier's support system.

As an Army wife, you have a lot of responsibilities and obligations. You are your soldier's support system and expected to be a pillar through separations, deployments and all that the Army tosses your way. But Army spouses are strong and resilient; that's what makes us so exceptional.

As a family, cooperate and stick together to make the soldier's transition easier. Research information about the customs of the military. Remember that each branch of the Armed Forces is different and you need to know specifically what to expect. A great place to start is with the Family Readiness Group, which is formed by men and women with loads of experience. Ask them for advice; they might have discovered new tricks or information that can help you out.

Army spouses are strong and resilient; that's what makes us so exceptional.

If you are the soldier, or in a dual military marriage as I was, remember to involve your spouse in as much of your military life as possible. Take him or her to any activity you can so he can get to know a little bit of what you do. If you are the military spouse, take advantage of any invitation that comes your way. Try to think of it as a window into his life, a privilege, not a duty.

DUAL CAREER MILITARY

Carlos and I were apart for most of our marriage. Our military training paths were completely different; he was at Fort Leonard Wood, Missouri, as a Combat Engineer, and I was in Fort Lee, Virginia, as a Quartermaster. We traveled to see each other every month and sometimes twice a month. Then he moved to Fort Benning, Georgia, and I moved to Fort Hood, Texas, to our respective units. Once we knew he would soon deploy, we didn't want to miss any opportunity to spend time together. That is important to remember; together time is vital to a successful marriage. We did not have any children, which made it easier for us when it came to quality time; we did not have to share it with anyone but each other.

Anyone with a loved one in the military needs to invest in a computer with a good video program!

Distance and separation is hard. I couldn't move to where he was, so we had to communicate and trust each other and coordinate visits as much as we could.

Anyone with a loved one in the military needs to invest in a computer with a good video program! The best thing, next to physically being in the same place at the same time, was calling each other using Skype or a messaging program with a video camera.

This makes it possible to see each other every day. Even though I couldn't reach out and hug Carlos, I could still look into his eyes, see his smile, talk and make future plans. The video programs are great tools—especially for kids when a parent is away!

MAKING A LIFE

MOVING ADVICE

Communicate!

Communication is what makes any relationship work; when in doubt, don't assume anything—ask. Moving is never easy, so a positive attitude is essential. Don't depend 100 percent on your spouse! He or she is extremely busy and can't be there 24/7 during the process.

Make a list noting who is responsible for each piece of the move; this will eliminate some of the angst. There is a transportation office on every post; use it and ask questions to get as much information as possible. If it's workable, visit your next duty station ahead of the move so you can ask more questions and familiarize yourself with the area. This will help ease the transition. The help is there, but if you don't ask you will never get it.

Discuss a tentative moving plan with your spouse so both of you know what has to happen and when. Establish some pre-moving tasks. For example, if you think you have too many things you don't need anymore, your spouse can go to the transportation office while you start making piles of what you can donate to a good cause or sell at a yard sale. Fewer things means an easier move—plus, donating items to charity will make you feel good.

With a move, as with everything in a marriage, it's very important to be a team! If you're not working together, you'll find yourself at odds with each other, and that's never a good way to begin somewhere new.

Once you are established at your new place, become part of the community and find things you enjoy doing in your downtime. Look for clubs you can join, start a hobby, find a job, volunteer or just do something that keeps you busy and makes you feel happy. I worked full time. Being a soldier is more than an eight-to-five job; there are long hours. I found activities outside my job that made me happy, which is really important. Those activities kept me in touch with myself as a woman and with reality outside the military world. Happy wife, happy life!

Also, get involved! Take advantage of the activities that are offered to you. Unite with fellow Army wives in everything you can. Even though I was also active duty, I found out that the Family Readiness Group (FRG) is there to offer constant support. You and your family need to connect with this team of amazing women and men. In times of sorrow they become a blanket of love and comfort.

That was exactly what they were to me; a very big blanket of love and comfort. Mrs. Love, the battalion commander's wife and president of the group, embraced her position with the FRG like a mother taking care of her children. She treated me like a daughter. Like any mother would do, she stood by me when I went through difficult times. Her unwavering persistence is why I was able to move forward with my life. I am forever grateful!

WHEN TRAGEDY STRIKES

I was getting my platoon ready for deployment at Fort Hood, Texas, when my commander called and asked me to meet him. I arrived at his office to find him with the battalion chaplain. Immediately I knew something was wrong, but I never imagined in a million years that I had lost my best friend, my husband. They were very kind in how they told me.

Carlos had gone to Iraq with the 3rd Infantry Division a year before I deployed. Although he was a Combat Engineer, he had prior service as an Infantryman. He was stationed in Baqubah, and he really liked to go on long patrols around the city. He would go on patrol for a couple of days straight, and then have a free day.

At lunch time on his free day, he went to the dining facility for a bite to eat. While he was waiting in line, an insurgent who had infiltrated the camp got in line behind him. The insurgent, who was wrapped in explosives, proceeded to detonate himself, taking the life of my husband and a civilian.

The only thing that gave me any peace was that the night before he died, we'd talked to each other online in a video chat using the camera. As we signed off, we said, "I love you." Those were the last words between us. At least I know he knew how I felt about him.

I was in total shock and disbelief. My commander and the chaplain asked if I had any local family to contact, but I didn't. They were all in Puerto Rico. I had a very good friend whom I called. He came at once, and we both cried for a long time. Then he stood by me and gave me strength to call my mother and then my mother-in-law.

Remember, it's okay to cry until there are no more tears. It's okay to be really angry, to talk only when you feel like it. You will not offend anybody when you use silence to try to understand your situation.

Always ask for help and never stay alone—not even when you feel like being alone. Finally, seek the help of a professional. Not everybody has experienced what you have. A professional can really help.

During this time, the Family Support Group of the unit helped me by bringing me dinner or lunch and lots of comfort cards. The way they reached out helped me *tremendously*.

Also, my commander told me that I didn't have to worry about anything. He was going to start the paperwork to finish my contract with the Army, but I asked him if I could stay. Many people asked why I chose to stay. I stayed because my husband and I were both in the Army because we loved it. We believed in the honor, potential and courage of the soldiers, and I didn't want to leave my platoon without a leader after we trained together for so long. My husband wouldn't have had it any other way either.

I went to Puerto Rico to receive his remains with our families and escorted the remains to the funeral home. Those days were very busy; we had a lot of friends and family that came to pay their respects. After a very beautiful funeral, the long, hard days started, but my family and friends helped me keep going. Keep family close during those times! Recovering from a death is tough. However, it's important to know (and to keep reminding yourself) that you can and will get past it.

Recognize that it's okay to have lots of different feelings. It's normal to feel sad, angry, exhausted, frustrated, and confused—and these feelings can be intense. You also may feel anxious about the future. Accept that reactions like these will lessen over time. Take time to heal.

Whatever you do, don't go through this alone! Sharing your feelings with friends and family can help get you through. Consider joining a support group where you can talk to others in similar situations. Do NOT isolate yourself, because if you do, your healing will only be delayed.

Get help if you need it. In the military, it's there 24/7! One place to seek help is Military OneSource. They will get all the information you need about anything you're looking for. The Family Readiness Group is another important source of support when you need people who will be there for you.

Everyone grieves differently, and the process takes time. There is no "normal" timetable for grieving. Whatever your situation, it's important to be patient with yourself.

GOLD STAR WIVES

When a loved one dies, we mostly need those we love around us. However, there is an organization that I also found to be crucial in helping to ease my pain and aid my healing process—Gold Star Wives. Gold Star Wives of America, Inc. is an organization of widows and widowers whose spouses died while on active duty or as the result of a military service–connected cause.

> There's something extraordinarily helpful about being in contact with a group of people who understand exactly what you're feeling.

While it's wonderful to be surrounded by people who love you, they can't really imagine what you're going through. So there's something extraordinarily helpful about being in contact with a group of people who understand exactly what you're feeling. Even if you're hesitant about reaching out to a group of strangers at one of the most vulnerable times in your life, do it. Trust me, they won't be strangers for long, and they will be of more help than you can imagine.

I have since left the Army, and I am now a make-up artist for models and fashion shows—a big difference from being a soldier. I will, however, always feel proud of my time, my duty, my country, and the honor of serving in the military. But most of all I will never forget the ultimate sacrifice my husband made for our great country.

PATTY MACEWEN

"After deployment, you will find a new normal."

When Patty MacEwen was a middle school student in Hampton, Virginia, she saw a drill demonstration by the high school Junior ROTC program. From that moment she was hooked, and in 1973 she was selected to be one of the first women in the JROTC program.

Patty joined ROTC while attending college. On finishing her master's degree, she attended the Army's Basic Course for Adjutant General officers. Adjutant General, or AG officers, are the personnel administrators for the Army. There she met her husband, David "Mac" MacEwen, who was also attending the AG Basic Course. Married for thirty years, they have two daughters, Lauren and Katie.

IN THE BEGINNING

During the first years of our marriage, Dave and I both served in the Army. Once I had my girls seventeen months apart, I knew it was time for me to get out. I didn't feel I could do the two things well, being a soldier and a mom. One or the other would suffer, and I didn't want either one not to be the best. Overall, I spent a total of five years and nine months as an Army officer.

I first got pregnant while Dave and I were attending our AG Advanced Course. I thought, "I'm not going to any more courses with *you*!" We met in the Basic Course, got pregnant in the Advanced Course, no telling *what* would have happened the next time!

So I went over to Korea pregnant with Lauren. We were still there when she was nine months old and I was having other symptoms.

Dave said, "You're pregnant again."

I said, "I can't be. I have a nine-month-old baby!"

But I was. So both my daughters were born while we were stationed in Korea.

I had my kids seventeen months apart, labored in the same hospital room, delivered in the same delivery room, and went through all of it without having any family around. That's one of the downsides of being stationed halfway around the world from home when you have a baby. You can talk to medical personnel, but you don't have family or girlfriends around to give you emotional support and "girl talk" advice.

My parents were also frustrated because they didn't get to see their first grandchild until she was nine months old. That was tough.

But the one really great thing about being in Korea is that when you need help around the house you can hire an *ajima* (like a professional grandma). Ours was wonderful. She would clean the house, do the laundry, and care for the baby. Picture someone who is so thorough she even irons your t-shirts and underwear before placing them back in the drawer!

Not only did she watch the baby during normal work hours, but if we were called out on a military alert at 4 a.m. she would come right away. Sometimes we would come home and Lauren would be fed, and all I would have to do is play with her and spend time with her, which was really nice.

The *ajima* made a very big difference. I don't think I could have done it without her, but it was still really difficult because I didn't feel like I had enough time off to be with the baby before going back to work. They only gave you four weeks back then. That was really hard. But I had very supportive bosses who always helped me if I needed to take the baby to the doctor for checkups or anything. And, best of all, my husband was always there for me!

MAKING A LIVING

THE "STICKER SHOCK" OF GOING FROM TWO INCOMES TO ONE

We left Korea after Kate was born, heading to Dave's next job, at the Pentagon. That was a really hard time, because I left the Army, which meant we went from two incomes to one.

We also bought a house in Woodbridge, Virginia. In hindsight, that was a mistake. With one salary, a mortgage and the cost of living in northern Virginia, we had no money. We couldn't afford babysitters or go out to dinner.

Dave was gone a lot, and I had two kids in diapers. That was not fun. Dave's job at the Pentagon was the "Korea Liaison," which meant he had weird hours, trying to be in the office at times when he could communicate with people in Korea. We didn't have traditional unit support, because we were not living on a military post. My folks were about three hours away.

I remember I got really, really sick one time. Dave was away somewhere, and my parents actually drove all the way up to get me and the girls and drove us back to their house to stay.

Needless to say, that was not my favorite time of life. It was such a drastic change to move away from the unit support in Korea, dual income, lower cost of living, and the personal time Dave and I had together. I wish I had been better prepared for the shock of all those changes.

ADJUSTING TO BEING A MOM

There was one other change I hadn't counted on. It is difficult adjusting to being a mommy after being a captain in the Army. No one recognizes you for anything. No one thanks you or says, "We are giving you this certificate of appreciation because you did this diaper so well." Not gonna happen!

It was so totally different from my former life, I struggled for awhile.

We moved from D.C. to Fort Hood, and Dave deployed for Desert Storm. When everyone was getting ready to deploy, I admit I was thinking, "This should be me! I should be going."

But if Dave and I had both been in, then we both would have gone to Saudi Arabia. I realized it would have been so hard on the girls, so I finally learned to adjust.

> **It is difficult adjusting to being a mommy after being a captain in the Army. No one recognizes you for anything. No one thanks you or says, "We are giving you this certificate of appreciation because you did this diaper so well."**

Dave was a big help. He kept saying, "You have the hardest job, staying stateside with the kids! It's easy to go away and go to work."

If it wasn't for him, it would have been a lot harder to get through the guilt of not deploying. The fact that I knew my kids needed me to be home—and that Dave wanted me to be home and thought that was as critical as him going away—made a big difference.

All told, this adjustment in my thinking took a good five years. It was a gradual shift in perspective. I used to feel more comfortable with men, in their world. I was not so into the typical interests of many women, the chatty sharing of stuff about kids. All that was foreign to me. When I finally made the shift and embraced where I was, knowing our girls would be better off with me there, it made a difference. I started to fit into my new role. Only then was I able to relax and discover that Fort Hood had a really good support system for me as a person and as a mom.

That support system was especially important when Dave deployed. Katie turned three the day we got to Fort Hood, and she was a real handful. I was looking for a preschool that would take Lauren and her. Someone told me about a local church that had a super preschool, and we got involved there. This provided both a great school for my girls and spiritual support. I got involved in a Bible study and also with "Moms in Touch," a special prayer group where I prayed with other moms for our children and their schools and their teachers. I have been a part of this program ever since. No matter where I have been, I always had someone to pray with. That spiritual support is key to making it through the tough times.

GETTING THROUGH DEPLOYMENT

Dave's deployment from Fort Hood to Desert Shield and Desert Storm with the Third Personnel Group was a hard time for me, but it was also a growing time. I learned a lot about myself and was probably better prepared for his next deployments to Kuwait, Albania, and finally into Iraq.

He did the smartest thing when he left with V Corps for Kuwait and Iraq. Dave looked at me and said, "Don't expect me back for a year."

Everyone else was saying, "Oh, it's gonna be a few months," but I kept what he said in mind. When they ended up staying longer than expected, I was prepared for it. Other spouses weren't. If you set your mind on a specific date your husband will return, you might be disappointed. Don't get stuck on a specific return date.

During his deployment with V Corps, we were stationed in Heidelberg, Germany. We had a great group of spouses at V Corps. We had great camaraderie, and everyone was so encouraging. In my housing area almost all of the guys were gone. I had a kiddie pool, so the wives would get together on my back porch, put our feet in the kiddie pool, drink margaritas, and listen to music. We called them "Pitty Pool Parties," but they were just good support. We all understood what each of us was going through. And we would find ways to help each other get through the difficult days.

> **If you set your mind on a specific date your husband will return, you might be disappointed. Don't get stuck on a specific return date.**

Keeping a good attitude is key for getting through a deployment. This is especially important with younger children who are not as understanding of things that are happening around them. If you need to cry, cry by yourself or cry with your friends, but try not to break down in front of your children, because that's hard for them. I think when the girls were older I might have broken down once or twice. But by then they could understand what was going on, why I was sad.

When they were little, I found a variety of ways to help the girls have fun supporting their Dad's deployment. We would do little cassette recordings of them reading and talking and goofing off and send them to him. The

Rear Detachment (the portion of the unit that remains back at home station with the families) had a special Valentine's Day event and we came all dressed in red, took pictures and then sent them to him. I think that was helpful. It helped the girls to know that Dad was getting those, and it helped him get through the deployment, too.

> If you need to cry, cry by yourself or cry with your friends, but try not to break down in front of your children, because that's hard for them.

DEPLOYMENT COMMUNICATION EXPECTATIONS

The first month of Operation Iraqi Freedom we had no contact with our husbands. I had a heads-up that this was coming, so I didn't let myself get all negative by worrying about it. My faith is everything, and it kept me positive. I said, "You know, he's in God's hands. I can't worry about it. Worrying will get me nowhere."

I didn't like not hearing from him, but I was okay, because I *knew* I wouldn't hear from him. I had the right expectations. If you expect to hear from you husband all the time, then you will be worried when you don't. My daughter Lauren's husband is deployed right now, and they Skype every day. We told them not to do that. Don't get on a regular schedule, because the moment one person is not there when you expect it, the other one gets all worried. But they can't help it; they are newlyweds, so they will just have to learn.

WATCHING THE NEWS

During Desert Shield and Desert Storm, every evening I would send the girls to bed and then watch the news. I would tape it and watch everything. I was really into it, glued to it, and that was not really helpful. It just made me keep wondering about what might be happening. Even though I had "let him go" in confidence that Dave was in God's care, it would still get me in a turmoil to watch the news. Lauren's husband told her not to watch the news while he's deployed, and she doesn't. She knows that if something happens that she really needs to know about, she will get the message.

STAY BUSY AND ASK FOR HELP

The best thing to do during a deployment is to keep yourself busy. I know it worked for me. When the girls were little, I was involved with their school. I ended up being the president of the Parent Teacher Organization and lots of other little things. Stay busy so you won't have a lot of downtime when you sit around just thinking.

Also, ask for help if you need it. A lot of people are afraid to ask for help.

I remember once when I had strep throat—I was really sick and needed help with the girls. I called a friend and said, "Can you please come?"

"Oh, I'll be happy to!" She had two boys about the same age. She picked up the girls and they spent the day at her house. I was able to get some rest.

When Dave was deployed to Iraq, a friend's brother-in-law came in from Italy to get some Lasik surgery done at Landstuhl hospital, which was about an hour away from our home in Heidelberg. I looked at him and said, "Would you please just give me a hug? I haven't had a "man hug" in so long." He laughed, and he gave me a hug. It is different. Hugs from the girls, your friends, are just different. You know, if you don't ask for help, you are not going to get it.

MAKING THE TOUGH DECISIONS

When we lived in Heidelberg my girls were in high school. In fact, Dave was deployed during Lauren's senior year. It was a lot of responsibility to decide what two female teens should be allowed to do without input from their father. I ended up making some decisions that Dave later told me he would not have agreed with at the time. But looking back, they were the right decisions.

"Mom, can I go out tonight downtown?" Lauren would ask. I know what's going to happen downtown, but she is going to go to college next year. So I would say, "Yeah, but call me. I want to know where you are." And she always did.

That's the kind of thing Dave probably would have said no to. But we had learned that the atmosphere in Germany was a little different than in the U.S. It was a safer environment for the kids. I recognized they could probably do more things than I might let them do back home. I think when the girls went to college, they had both "been there, done that," and didn't feel like college was the great opportunity to try everything they had not been allowed to do before.

POST-DEPLOYMENT REUNION

After deployment, don't expect to get back to normal right away. You will find a new normal. When Dave was gone, I took over the finances. Before, he used to do them by himself. When he returned from deployment and saw how I had handled them, he liked that. Now we do them together. It's our new normal.

Don't expect the relationship to get back just like it was right away. Be excited that he is coming home, but be yourself. I know a lot of people, even some who have been married for a while, who get all spun up thinking, "Oh, has he changed? Have I changed? What's going on?"

> After deployment, don't expect to get back to normal right away. You will find a new normal.

Just be who you are now. It will be okay. Deployments and separation do change you, but they also make you both stronger.

MAKING A LIFE

DAY TO DAY SECRETS

Be organized, but don't get too far ahead of yourself.

For me right now, focusing on the present is really important. I'm doing stuff that relates to my husband's unit, stuff that relates to the installation; people are retiring, people are leaving, and if I am not keeping up with my schedule I am going to miss something. It is easy to get confused. So I must survive day to day by just remembering to "be in the present."

> **A lot of being in the Army is waiting for the next thing. But you must be mindful of the present, where you are today**

A lot of being in the Army is waiting for the next thing. But you must be mindful of the present, where you are today, instead of thinking about *Oh, next week Dave's gotta go on a trip here* or *Where are we going to be next year?* or *When is he going to get his next promotion? What is the next job going to be?*

Just focus on the here and now. Be in the moment.

Be involved, but do as much as *you* want to. Do what you are comfortable with. Don't do what you think other people want you to do. Stay busy, but not too busy. Have a balanced life. Home, work, kids, spiritual, physical, all that. You've got to take care of yourself before you can take care of anybody else.

MOVING AND SETTLING IN

Coming here to Fort Jackson was my twentieth move in thirty years of marriage. You'd think I know everything by now. Really, what helps most is to have a master list of all the things you have to do. Have a list of all the bills and all the magazines that will need a change of address. If you have to do the water, electric or trash, have that on the list. Changing doctors and getting your medical records should be on the master list. It's the same every time, so get organized and make a list.

Our family makes it a point to unpack quickly. It can help to schedule something that keeps you from dragging your feet. On our most recent move, we received our household goods

On our most recent move, we received our household goods on Monday and scheduled a reception at our home for the next Saturday. This forced us to unpack fast.

on Monday and scheduled a reception at our home for the next Saturday. This forced us to unpack fast. It would be tempting to just do so much and then say, "Oh, I'll get to that later," but we had people coming for a big event, so we kept working and got it done.

Another secret we didn't learn until more recently: when the movers unpack you, have one place set aside, like the garage or a separate room, where boxes go when you are not sure about their final destination. Then you can go into that room and move things out as you have time, and the rest of your house doesn't feel crunched and cluttered. You will feel a little more settled, quickly.

One way I help myself settle into a new community is to drive around and get lost. Seriously. Because when I just drive around and say, "Let's see where this road goes," I find more shortcuts and different places. Eventually that's how I learn my way around.

When setting up a house or apartment, be creative. We have lived in many different kinds and sizes of places. In Germany, we had a teeny, teeny kitchen. We called it a "one-butt kitchen." I went to IKEA, bought a shelf, and put it in the kitchen. That's where everything went: pots and pans and everything.

In Texas, we used plastic bottle six-pack holders to channel curtain valances. I had friends who used fabric on their walls like wallpaper. We used a closet as a pantry. You can complain that you don't have all the space or the right rooms to set up your household, or you can be creative with what you are given. Make do with what you have, and have fun with it.

CHILDREN AND FREQUENT MOVES

There are a lot of programs available to help support your children as you move from place to place. My girls were involved in Club Beyond (part of the Military Community Youth Ministry), youth activities, sports, and trips in Germany. Take advantage of what's offered and get the kids involved.

But moving will still be hard. It was more difficult for our girls as they got older. Lauren, our oldest, was in three high schools in three years. One year we were in a little place in Germany with a small school that included seventh through twelfth grades. Everybody was friends. No cliques, everyone got along. They had the best year.

Then we moved to Newport, Rhode Island, and Lauren went to Rogers High School, which was a large public high school. Katie adjusted better, because she got involved in soccer and theater. She also made a good friend.

Meanwhile, Lauren painted her nails black, dyed her hair dark, and didn't really get involved in school. It was a really hard year for her. The kids on Fort Adams, where we lived during that time, offered some support. There wasn't a lot we could do for her except wait it out.

The next year we moved back to Germany, and she was fine. The upside to all this moving was that once the girls graduated from high school, and it was time for them to go to college, I wasn't worried about them. They had done so many things, met so many people, adjusted so many times, I knew they wouldn't have any problems. And they really didn't.

EMBRACE WHERE YOU ARE

Every place we have been has had its own unique atmosphere and culture, and we have loved all of them. When we were in Texas, we loved to do all the Texas stuff: cowboy boots, barbeque, whatever. In Newport, Rhode Island, we were right on the water, and since Dave was a student at the Naval War College, we could spend quality time together. When we lived at Fort Myer, Virginia, we were right outside of Arlington National Cemetery. The Caissons went by my window every morning and afternoon. I could look out my kitchen window and see the honor guards. It was so beautiful and moving to walk through the cemetery.

Korea, Germany—each unique location has a special place in our hearts. Wherever you are, embrace the culture, enjoy the community.

BEWARE OF UNREALISTIC EXPECTATIONS

Not every Army wife has the same level of interest in her husband's unit, and that is okay. Some wives are very involved in their spouses' units and careers. If you are one of those, don't think you can do it all. Even if you want to do it all, you can't. Other spouses may want to be less involved or have their own jobs. The Army is more accepting these days of spouses who are doing their own thing, and that's good. So don't expect that every married soldier will have a spouse who is ready to jump in and help with unit activities.

For the first six years of my marriage, I was Army. I didn't know anything about spouse things. I didn't go through the Army Family Team Building program. I didn't do any of the initial Army spouse events. Then boom, we were in Fort Hood, and the Family Readiness Groups (FRGs) were starting up for the first time, and the unit was preparing to deploy. I was expected to help the battalion FRG, but no one knew what we were supposed to be doing! It was a really confusing time. I had to learn to manage my own expectations, and not get upset by unrealistic expectations put on me by others.

So do what *you* are comfortable with. If you really want to support the unit and get out there and be involved, do it. It you don't want to do as much, then try to be involved somehow, even if it is just a little bit.

ADVICE TO A FRIEND

Anyone joining the military will soon learn that it is like a huge family. Take advantage of that. Take advantage of the many things the military has to offer, like Armed Forces Vacation Club, military discounts, and MWR (Morale, Welfare, and Recreation) trips. These may not be the most critical things in life, but they are perks you should embrace. Enjoy them while you can.

> The family isn't going to come first for someone in the Army. It's just a fact of life. The mission is critical. The mission will always come first.

Another tip for new families to absorb is that even though you often hear people say, "Put your family first," in reality, the family isn't going to come first for someone in the Army. It's just a fact of life. The mission is critical. The mission will always come first. If it is your expectation that every time your kid has an important baseball game or concert your husband will leave work and come to that event, you are going to be disappointed. He can't always do that. If you don't accept that, it is going to cause tension. His job really does come first, so make peace with waiting.

Also, it is not only the soldier who is forced to "hurry up and wait!"

Spouses also face this. When husbands are deployed, you are waiting, waiting. Wondering about the next assignment, you are waiting, waiting. Dave would come home and say, "Oh, I think we are going to move to this location." Then soon it was, "Oh, no, I think we're gonna go here, instead." After another "No, wait . . . we might be . . . ," I finally said, "When you really know, tell me. I am not going to believe you until you show me the orders on paper and I will know we are really going there."

Make peace with waiting. Just be in the present, and enjoy where you are. Enjoy the Army life. It is really unique. It is a great brotherhood and sisterhood, and there is nothing like it in the world.

Make peace with waiting. Just be in the present, and enjoy where you are. Enjoy the Army life. It is really unique. It is a great brotherhood and sisterhood, and there is nothing like it in the world.

Don't be scared. There are people out there who will help you. You may feel like you are not going to do things the right way, but there is always going to be somebody to ask, or even just watch. I pay attention to people so I can learn how to act and what to do. Pick people that you admire, people who seem to know what they are doing, and emulate them. Model them, or ask them, "Hey, what do I do about this?"

You could beat yourself up wondering *What am I supposed to do?*—but all you really have to do is ask. People want to help.

BEING THE WIFE OF A GENERAL

Not long ago my husband was selected to be a brigadier general. After he was promoted, I got some very helpful advice: because you are a general officer's spouse, people pay more attention to what you say. People assume you know what you are talking about, so be very careful not to put out wrong information. So now I try to watch what I say, because people will assume I know a lot more than I really do. I'm learning to say, "You know what? I don't know. Can I get back to you on that?"

When you are a general's spouse, you always end up sitting at the head table at banquets. I'm not used to being at a head table. Remember what I said about watching others to learn what to do? Now junior people are watching me so they will know what to do. That's a little scary! I really want to do the right thing.

Dave and I make it a priority to communicate and synchronize our calendars. There are a lot of events that my husband is expected to attend, and it is very important for us to talk about these events and decide which ones I will attend. He categorizes them for me: the events and things he really wants me to attend, the events and things he would like me to attend, and the events and things I should only attend if I really want to. This helps me to prioritize. I can't do it all, even though I'd like to sometimes. But then, I just don't have the energy to do all of those things. So when we communicate, I know his expectations and can focus my energy on the right activities.

In Dave's current position we do a lot of entertaining. I think this is common for most general officers, and we actually love to do it. We feel like our quarters here on the military post are not our private space but something we want everyone to come and enjoy. One week we might have a group of warrant officers from the AG School over for chips and dip and an informal chat. The next week it might be a delegation of senior officers from Jordan, and we hire a caterer and offer a much more formal setting.

In preparing to host international visitors, I have found it helpful to research their culture, foods and current events. Knowing these things, I felt more confident in my interactions with them.

FINAL THOUGHTS

I remember talking with my best friend when we were at our ROTC Basic Course summer camp in 1977. We met to chat one day, and I said, "You know what, I don't know if I will stay in the Army, but I always want to be associated somehow with the Army." Little did I know that I would marry a soldier—but I like it! There are so many things I like about the Army. I love ceremonies and all that tradition. I love all of the places I have been. I wouldn't change a thing. Even though sometimes there are ups and sometimes there are downs, most of the time Dave and I look at each other in amazement and say, "Can you believe where we are?"

APPENDICES

SIXTEEN WAYS TO HELP MILITARY FAMILIES FEEL APPRECIATED

HELP WITH SIMPLE CHORES

Mow a lawn, shovel a drive, deliver a meal the day our soldier leaves for training, the field, or a deployment. Sometimes, simple chores fall to the wayside during stressful times without the soldier. These small acts have a big impact on a military family living outside of their installation.

WRITE TO US

Send our kids letters. We often live far away from family and they love to get mail. It makes them feel important and lets them know you care. Don't write about the deployment, it's especially good if you write about other things. On the other hand, don't be too over-bearing. Too many gifts or too many interruptions to kids' routine can make day to day life difficult for the parent holding down the fort.

WELCOME US INTO THE NEIGHBORHOOD

Military families are always on the move. Instead of counting us out since you know we'll be moving on, go out of your way to welcome us to the community. Make up a small welcome basket and include maps and a list of some of your favorite places for shopping, hair, nails, and places of interest. Anything to help in a families' transition is greatly appreciated.

LISTEN TO US

Sometimes military spouses just need to vent. Listen to us. It's okay for us to be angry and upset that our spouse is gone. It's hard to do it all alone and keeping it inside just makes it worse. Don't respond by saying things like, "put on a brave face" or, "you'd better not share this with your spouse. "

BE A FRIEND

If a spouse is deployed, be a friend. This is a tough time for any family, but those separated by deployments are more at risk for depression. Being alone is difficult. An invitation to dinner or even just to spend some time to connect at whatever level is greatly appreciated. This is especially true during holiday seasons. If a family can't get "home," for whatever reason, include them in holiday parties or celebrations. Invite them to share Christmas dinner or New Year's Eve with you.

BABYSIT OR PLAN A SHOPPING TRIP

Offer to babysit so the at-home spouse can have some "me time" or can just go shopping. Alternatively, offer to shop with a spouse during the holidays. This way the parent can shop and you could help with the child. Two adults are always better than one when shopping. This also is dual purpose in that company is always appreciated.

Family Night Package

Put together a "family night package" for families of those deployed. I love making "family movie night" packages for my friends who didn't get to go home to visit during the holidays. I filled a popcorn bowl with popcorn, snacks, and a movie. It shows you're thoughtfulness and shows the family you are thinking of them. Be sure to make it as personal as possible (age appropriate movie for kids, etc.) .

UNEXPECTED DINNER

Drop off a dinner for the family of a deployed soldier at their doorstep "just because," without the expectation of coming in for a long chat.

FRIENDS' NIGHT OUT

If the spouse is a friend, just go over to visit or pick her up for a night out, even when she protests that she has other things to do. Be helpful. Don't tell her you understand, because you don't, and don't wait for her to ask for help, because she usually won't.

HIRE HER!

Are you a business owner? Hire a military spouse even though you know she will likely move in a couple of years. She needs to have her own identity, and she needs marketable skills. Also, go out of your way to hire a vet!

ADD YOUR WELCOME

If you live near a military installation, be part of the crowd who welcomes soldiers home or wishes them well as they leave.

ASK

Ask a military wife what she needs from you. Different families need different support. Then don't be surprised when we take you up on your offer.

Pray

Pray every night for the soldiers and their families.

MILITARY APPRECIATION NIGHT

Restaurants, corporations, or anyone who plans local events: have a military appreciation night to honor those who keep us free. It is because of our military we can attend these events without fear.

SEE A SOLDIER?

Thank him or her for their many sacrifices in support of our country. Shake his or her hand whether at the airport, on the street or at a restaurant. Thank you means so much to them. If you are financially able, pay for a meal, buy them lunch, can be in person or anonymously.

APPRECIATE THE WIFE

It is important to not only tell the service member how much their service is appreciated, but telling a spouse is also important. They are essential for a stable home life. Have you heard the phrase "Happy Wife, happy life?"

COMMONLY USED ABBREVIATIONS

AAFES	Army And Air Force Exchange Service	
ACS	Army Community Services	Provides services for families
ACU	Army Combat Uniform	
AER	Army Emergency Relief	
AFTB	Army Family Team Building	
AG	Adjutant General	
AGR	Active Guard Reserve	Full-time job supporting National Guard or Army Reserve
AIT	Advanced Individual Training	Specialty training after basic training
ALC	Advanced Leader Course	2nd course in NCOES
APFT	Army Physical Fitness Test	
APO	Army Post Office	Handles mail for Soldiers overseas
ARNG	Army National Guard	
ASU	Army Service Uniform	The new dress blue uniform
AWOL	Absent Without Leave	
BAH	Basic Allowance for Housing	The portion of your pay that goes to housing
BDE	Brigade	
BLUF	Bottom Line Up Front	The most important information a leader needs
BN	Battalion	
BOQ	Bachelor Officers' Quarters	
CAC	Common Access Card	A "smart ID" card for military and civilian DoD employees
CDR	Commander	
CO	Commanding Officer	
CONUS	Continental United States	Does not include Alaska and Hawaii
CSA	Chief of Staff of the Army	Most senior officer in the Army

DA	Department of the Army	
DEERs	Defense Enrollment Eligibility System	Computerized database of military families that establishes eligibility for insurance
DEROS	Date of Estimated Return from Overseas	The date your overseas tour is scheduled to end
DFAC	Dining Facility	Military cafeteria (also called "Mess Hall")
DITY	Do it Yourself Move	Move your own household goods instead of using a professional shipper
DIV	Division	
DoD	Department of Defense	
EFMP	Exceptional Family Member Program	Mandatory enrollment to ensure family members with special medical or educational needs receive the proper housing and care.
ETS	Estimated Time of Separation	The day you will get out of the Army if you don't reenlist
FRG	Family Readiness Group	Unit support group for families
FRSA	Family Readiness Support Assistant	Employee who helps provide administrative assistance for FRGs
FTX	Field Training Exercise	Also called "going to the field"
GO	General Officer	
HMMWV	High-Mobility Multi-purpose Wheeled Vehicle	(Pronounced "Humvee") common source for transportation
IMCOM	Installation Management Command	
JAG	Judge Advocate General	Military lawyers
JMTC	Joint Multinational Training Center	Training center located in Grefenwoeher, Germany
JRTC	Joint Readiness Training Center	Training center in Ft. Polk, LA
KIA	Killed in Action	
LES	Leave and Earnings Statement	The pay voucher
LZ	Landing Zone	

M16/M4	Rifles currently carried by Army soldiers	
MIA	Missing in Action	
MOS	Military Occupational Specialty	Job classification
MRE	Meals Ready to Eat	Field Rations
MWR	Morale, Welfare, and Recreation	
9mm	(Pronounced "nine-mil")	Pistol often carried by officers and some NCOs
NCO	Noncommissioned Officer	
NCOES	Non-Commissioned Officer Education System	
NTC	National Training Center	Training center located in Ft. Irwin, CA
OCONUS	Outside Continental United States	Includes Alaska and Hawaii
PAO	Public Affairs Officer	Handles media relations for the Army
PCS	Permanent Change of Station	Move to a new assignment
POC	Point of Contact	
PT	Physical Training	
PX	Post Exchange	Variety store on a post or base
RD	Rear Detachment	
R&R	Rest and Recreation	Leave, often taken as break from a deployment
ROTC	Reserve Officer Training Corps	College-based program to train military officers
SF	Special Forces	Army's experts in unconventional warfare
SGLI	Soldiers Group Life Insurance	
SLC	Senior Leader Course	3rd Course in NCOES

SMA	Sergeant Major of the Army	Most senior enlisted person in the Army
SOP	Standard Operating Procedure	
TDY	Temporary Duty Assignment	Work-related trip
TRICARE	Military health care system	
VCSA	Vice Chief of Staff of the Army	2nd most senior officer in the Army
WIA	Wounded in action	
WLC	Warrior Leader Course	1st course in NCOES
XO	Executive Officer	

RANKS

Insignia	Pay Grade	Name	Abbreviation
ENLISTED			
None	E-1	Private	PVT
	E-2	Private 2	PV2
	E-3	Private First Class	PFC
	E-4	Specialist	SPC
	E-4	Corporal	CPL
	E-5	Sergeant	SGT
	E-6	Staff Sergeant	SSG
	E-7	Sergeant First Class	SFC
	E-8	Master Sergeant	MSG
	E-8	First Sergeant	1SG
	E-9	Sergeant Major	SGM
	E-9	Command Sergeant Major	CSM
	E-9 (special)	Sergeant Major of the Army	SMA
WARRANT OFFICERS			
	W-1	Warrant Officer	WO1

	W-2	Chief Warrant Officer 2	CW2
	W-3	Chief Warrant Officer 3	CW3
	W-4	Chief Warrant Officer 4	CW4
	W-5	Chief Warrant Officer 5	CW5
OFFICERS			
	O-1	2nd Lieutenant	2LT
	O-2	1st Lieutenant	1LT
	O-3	Captain	CPT
	O-4	Major	MAJ
	O-5	Lieutenant Colonel	LTC
	O-6	Colonel	COL
	O-7	Brigadier General	BG
	O-8	Major General	MG
	O-9	Lieutenant General	LTG
	O-10	General	GEN

MILITARY TIME

Civilian Time	Army Time	How they Pronounce It
1:00 a.m.	0100	Zero-One-Hundred
2:00 a.m.	0200	Zero-Two-Hundred
3:00 a.m.	0300	Zero-Three-Hundred
4:00 a.m.	0400	Zero-Four-Hundred
5:00 a.m.	0500	Zero-Five-Hundred
6:00 a.m.	0600	Zero-Six-Hundred
7:00 a.m.	0700	Zero-Seven-Hundred
8:00 a.m.	0800	Zero-Eight-Hundred
9:00 a.m.	0900	Zero-Nine-Hundred
10:00 a.m.	1000	Ten-Hundred
11:00 a.m.	1100	Eleven-Hundred
12:00 p.m.	1200	Twelve-Hundred
1:00 p.m.	1300	Thirteen-Hundred
2:00 p.m.	1400	Fourteen-Hundred
3:00 p.m.	1500	Fifteen-Hundred
4:00 p.m.	1600	Sixteen-Hundred
5:00 p.m.	1700	Seventeen-Hundred
6:00 p.m.	1800	Eighteen-Hundred
7:00 p.m.	1900	Nineteen-Hundred
8:00 p.m.	2000	Twenty-Hundred
9:00 p.m.	2100	Twenty-One-Hundred
10:00 p.m.	2200	Twenty-Two-Hundred
11:00 p.m.	2300	Twenty-Three-Hundred
12:00 a.m.	2400	Twenty-Four-Hundred

A few sample times		
9:30 a.m.	0930	Zero-Nine-Thirty
10:45 a.m.	1045	Ten-Forty-Five
2:15 p.m.	1415	Fourteen-Fifteen
11:08 p.m.	2308	Twenty-Three-Oh-Eight

ARMY UNITS

UNIT	SIZE*	RANK of Senior Enlisted	RANK of Commander
Squad	10	Staff Sergeant ("Squad Leader")	
Platoon	40	Sergeant First Class ("Platoon Sergeant")	1st Lieutenant
Company	175	First Sergeant ("Top")	Captain
Battalion	700	Command Sergeant Major	Lieutenant Colonel
Brigade	4,500+	Command Sergeant Major	Colonel
Division	15,000+	Command Sergeant Major	Major General
Corps	30,000+	Command Sergeant Major	Lieutenant General

*Sizes are approximate and will vary depending on the type of unit.

Helpful Resources

MyPay (Defense Finance and Accounting System): https://mypay.dfas.mil/	Manage allotments, get leave and earnings statements, travel pay
IMCOM (Installation Management Command) http://www.imcom.army.mil/	Find information about your next Army post.
MWR (Morale, Welfare, and Recreation) http://www.armymwr.com/	Information about recreational opportunities
DPS (Defense Personal Property System) http://www.move.mil/	Help plan to move your household goods
Army OneSource http://www.myarmyonesource.com/	Army family programs and services
Military OneSource http://www.militaryonesource.mil/	Military family programs and services
TRICARE http://www.tricare.mil/	Military medical insurance plan
EFMP Resources http://efmp.amedd.army.mil/	What EFMP (Exceptional Family Member Program) is and how to enroll

ORGANIZATIONS

- Adopt a soldier through various organizations such as ADOPT A SOLDIER, or OPERATION ADOPT A SOLDIER, or Soldiers Angels. This can help children and family become involved and is a great way to teach our children to give of themselves.

- Don't forget the families. MILITARYKIDS.ORG is a great organization that sends military kids to camp, spa gift cards for spouses, etc.

- Check out GUARDIAN ANGELS FOR SOLDIER'S PET (www.guardianangelsforsoldierspet.org). Donate to the cause or go the extra mile and apply to foster a deployed soldier's pet.

- Become involved in RIDE 2 RECOVERY (www .ride2recovery.com). This organization provides bicycles to wounded warriors, from ordinary bikes for those with PTSD to modified bikes for soldiers missing limbs. From donating to participating in a ride to volunteering as a nurse for a weeklong event, there are many options to become involved.

- Donate your time and/or money to military causes that help injured members. There are so many great ones out there such as WOUNDED WARRIORS or organizations in your hometown.

ACKNOWLEDGEMENTS

The Army community is famous for its willingness to expend time and energy in support of its families. The authors were the beneficiaries of that attitude, as people stepped up to provide critical resources and advice to us. We are thankful for Nancy Lembke, wife of a senior leader in the Army Chaplain Corps, who provided a very significant contribution after viewing advance copies of the first two Now You Tell Me! books. "You need to write one about Army wives!" was her immediate reaction. Well Nancy, here it is! We also acknowledge Leslie Love, with multiple tours as commander's spouse and FRG leader, whose warm heart and infectious laugh have endeared her to countless Army spouses over the years. Her connections enabled us to include some very important stories in this book.

We thank all 12 (13?) Army wives for sharing their personal and touching stories and experiences. You are certainly all great role models who exhibited such strong and resilient strength in being a special part of the Army family. We send a special thank you to Nancy Negron, for sharing her painful, yet beautiful, love story about her husband, First Lieutenant Carlos J. Diaz Santiago, who was killed in action while serving our country.

Finally, the acknowledgements for this book would be incomplete unless we recognized all the multi-tasking, budget building, child chauffeuring, menu planning, home decorating Army spouses who not only support their own soldiers, but also reach out without hesitation to assist any member of the military community who needs a hand. Well done! As the 38th Chief of Staff, Army General Ray Odierno says, "The Strength of our Nation is our Army, The Strength of our Army is our Soldiers, The Strength of our Soldiers is our Families, This is what makes us "Army Strong".

m

ABOUT THE AUTHORS

SHERIDAN SCOTT, the primary author of the *Now You Tell Me!* series, has edited half a dozen Chicken Soup for the Soul books as well as served as a Chicken Soup co-author. An award winning biographer, she has been a staff writer for five national magazines and has ghostwritten for dozens of celebrities as well as hundreds of regular folks.

B.K. SHERER is the best-selling author of the riveting Eden Thrillers series, which she co-authored with friend and fellow writer, Sharon Linnéa.

B. K. holds a Master of Divinity degree from Princeton Theological Seminary and a doctorate from Oklahoma State University. A Presbyterian minister, she currently serves on active duty as a chaplain in the United States Army. Her work has taken her to Argentina, Somalia, Korea, Costa Rica, Germany, Kuwait and Iraq.

DONNA LYONS is a military news journalist and author based in Washington, D.C. Donna has published articles in *Military News, Defense News, Veterans Affairs, Military Communities, Army Special Forces, Navy SEALs, Law Enforcement, WWII Veterans,*

Female Service Members and *International Military Travel*, along with two weekly columns for Examiner.com. Her writing has concentrated on the wars in Iraq and Afghanistan, highlighting the positive aspects of individuals, projects and programs that benefit our military, veterans, wounded warriors and their families. She offers a nonpartisan and inspiring journalistic view, working in tandem with numerous veterans and military organizations. Donna has three adult children, Brooke, Britt and Nick, and a grandson, Sean Riley; they are a very proud military family.

Originally from Huntington Beach, California, Donna currently resides in Alexandria, Virginia. She can be reached via email at Author1@live.com.

A portion of the proceeds from the sale of this book will go to support Army wives. For more information go to www.arundelpublishing.com

For more information,
resources and to join these
and other army wives in conversation visit
www.nowyoutellmebooks.com/armywives